EVERYDAY
CYBERSECURITY

EVERYDAY

CYBERSECURITY

A practical approach to understanding cybersecurity, security awareness, and protecting your personal information and identity.

Christopher K. Cox

Cover by Stephen C. Cox

Edited by Kaitlyn S. Hedges.

ISBN-13: 978-1-7330186-0-9

Dedication

First, and foremost, this book is dedicated to my wonderful wife, Esther. She has listened to me for years about my desire to write books. When the opportunity for this book came up, she was supportive and encouraging, even when the book consumed Saturdays, evenings, and some vacation time to complete. She is my biggest cheerleader.

This is also dedicated to my parents, who stoked my initial desires to write by reading my first books, way back in second grade. While I liked writing, they planted the seed of becoming a published author.

Acknowledgements

A big thanks goes to my brother, Steve, who created the cover for this book. When I talked to him about what I was looking for, he came up with this look, which is better than what I was thinking of.

I also want to acknowledge the hard work of my editor, Kaitlyn Hedges. She took my work and polished it up. Her eye for detail definitely caught things I had missed. I did add some things after she finished, so I may have introduced more errors.

Finally, I need to express my appreciation to the professors in my masters of cybersecurity program: Robert M. Jorgensen, Basil Hamdan, and C. Paul Morrey. They expanded on my previous experience and knowledge, and introduced me to new ones. Professor Jorgensen was particularly encouraging of this book.

Contents

Author's Foreword

A couple of years after I started working as an IT technician, I began an undergraduate program in information systems. One of the classes I took was on information security. The topic intrigued me.

At the time, I was fairly new as the IT "expert" in my department. There were times during those first years when blank stares were returned as I tried to explain something, usually because I'd use the technical terminology I was learning in classes. To me, I sounded like I knew what I was doing. Even in my writing, such as emails to staff, I often used the more technical terms. It took some time for me to realize I wasn't helping anyone with the techno-talk.

One of my directors told me, on more than one occasion, I needed to remember that most of the people I worked with were used to big buttons to push and levers to pull. It was his way of telling me to keep things simple and communicate at a level others understand.

I'm not perfect at it, but I've gotten better over 10+ years at learning to simplify techno-jargon.

One of my recurring thoughts over the years, especially during my master's program, has been how I can better help non-technical people be more security minded, without being too technical. Sometimes the technical terms are needed and need to be understood. However, too often people get lost in the alphabet-soup of acronyms and terminology.

When it comes to security, people are generally the weakest link, the most susceptible to failure, and the most likely to facilitate a data breach (often unintentionally). That is where the seeds to this book started.

My main intent with this book is to focus on the most important parts of cybersecurity, increase your awareness, and help you on your path to better security and data privacy. It's not an end-all discussion in cybersecurity, nor will it cover every aspect of cybersecurity.

As we go through the information, you may be surprised by the number of physical security practices discussed. Keep in mind, our real, physical lives are greatly affected by our virtual security, and physical security practices can also affect our cybersecurity.

Whenever possible, I have tried to use generic identifiers when referring to a person, such as a hacker. However, unless referring to a specific individual, I will sometimes use "he" or "she" interchangeably.

What you read and apply in your digital (and even physical) world can make your personal security stronger. To further strengthen your own and others' cyber identity, I suggest taking what you learn and sharing it with others—family, friends, coworkers.

Helping others become more security conscious also helps protect your data, particularly if any of your family, friends, or coworkers have access to any part of your digital identity, including social media, email, and other web locations. Increasing their security awareness and practices strengthens the security chain that keeps your data safer.

If you do find this book helpful, please let others know by telling them about it and leaving a review.

Who Is This Book for?

This book is not a "textbook" or filled with techno-jargon. Tech terms will be used, but I'll try to explain them in simple, common language. My goal is to provide you with an essential, foundational understanding of cybersecurity.

This book is specifically for non-technical users who want to increase the security of their personal information. It's not necessarily a "how-to" book because computers, devices, and programs are constantly changing, and there's no way a single book could cover every cybersecurity scenario. It's more of the "what" and "why" behind cybersecurity, and having better security awareness.

However, this book can also be useful for technical users. Technical users who may find this book useful include those who:

- Don't know much about cybersecurity and want to gain a better understanding of security issues.
- Want to share an easy-to-understand cybersecurity awareness resource.
- Need help speaking at a commonly understood level.

Most of the people I know are non-technical users. By this, I mean they use computers, but they aren't "IT" people. Beyond installing a program by clicking "Next," "Next," and "Finish" and maybe customizing their computer with a background and some personalization, they're unfamiliar with configuring systems and troubleshooting problems.

In over 11 years of technical support, I've found most people would actually like to solve their own problems. Most want to be more cyber-aware and secure. Many think they're "dumb," but in my experience, we could all be considered "dummies" in something, but nobody wants to be dumb.

We need someone to talk in a language we understand and guide us through the process of understanding the unfamiliar. I can learn something from anyone, and I'll probably feel dumb when I'm learning from someone else's expertise.

I've seen eyes glaze over when an IT person speaks techno-talk to a non-technical user. Users would rather the IT "expert" take over in solving a computer problem because they believe most computer problems are too difficult to fix. And, most IT people just take over, because it's easier and quicker for everyone.

Unfortunately, while it is easier for the tech to do this, it also perpetuates the idea that regular computer users aren't able, or smart enough, to do things themselves.

This false perception also applies to information security.

While most computer users believe computer security is important, most also fail to do what is necessary to be more secure, usually because they don't know what to do. Often the failure happens when they think implementing better security will be harder or too inconvenient.

Certainly, most IT (and cybersecurity) professionals continue this perception by implementing security processes and procedures that often complicate things beyond what is necessary. In addition, the professionals often don't help users understand the reasons for the security processes.

Admittedly, implementing security can add a layer of complexity, and it may reduce the ease and convenience most users (even in IT and security) would prefer.

However, being secure doesn't have to be hard. It begins with awareness and incorporating practices that make it harder for the bad guys to get your information.

As an extension to cybersecurity, sections of this book also reference physical security. A lot of real-life security habits tend to correlate to our cybersecurity attitude. Although the physical counterparts to our digital information are often overlooked, they also need to be secure.

There are many computer security books and other resources available. I've found most books to be too technical for the average computer user. Not that the user can't learn, but they just don't want to take the time and effort to learn the deeper ins and outs because it's not relevant to them. A lot of online resources tend to focus on single aspects of cybersecurity. In this book, I wanted to combine a lot of essential information into a single resource.

Most people know they're supposed to be more security-aware. However, cybersecurity is a nebulous concept to many, and, other than passwords, a lot of people don't really understand that security involves everything they do with computing devices.

Hopefully, you will gain a greater understanding of cybersecurity as some of the why's and how's are explained.

CHAPTER 1

You Are the Target

Even if you think you aren't, you are the target.

You may not be the only target, but you are a target of cybercriminals.

Maybe you're not an executive of a company. Maybe you're not worth multiple millions of dollars. But . . .

You are the target.

So, what do you have that is of worth to the cybercriminals? Here are four areas of value.

First, do you have a bank account? What about a credit card? The bad guys don't care how little you have; they're just as willing to wipe it clean for you whether you have $5 or millions.

Second, do you use a computing device? Computer? Mobile device? Something that connects to the internet? I'll explain in a minute why that's of value.

Third, do you have any contacts? These could be email contacts, address book contacts, and social media contacts. Who might these contacts consist of? Family, friends, coworkers, and even people you have never personally met but have added as "friends" to your Facebook, LinkedIn, or other social media account(s).

Fourth, do you have any kind of identity? Driver's license? Social Security number? Government or other official identification? What about access to an organization's computing system? What about the

1

identities of family members? There's a big market for identity theft and fraud.

These are just four of the general reasons (and they're not all the reasons) you are a target. Let's look a little more closely at each of these.

Your bank account is probably the more obvious target. Other financial accounts—credit cards, investing accounts—are also targets. Even if these accounts have no money in them, they are a source of identity information, which we'll discuss more in a little bit.

A lot of people don't realize your computing devices are targets. Other than a thief selling the electronic device, if your device has business, confidential, or proprietary information on it—including intellectual property, patent details, trade secrets—it has value as competitive advantage, as extortion/blackmail, or to foreign nations looking to exploit the market.

Though most of us don't have this level of information on our devices, hackers will still collect passwords, personal files, and other data off your computer.

Years ago, it seemed most malware was destructive in nature, where it might erase your files. But hackers have learned there is value in information. Besides stealing data, certain types of malware will lock up your files until you pay a ransom to unlock them. Many people will pay to restore the only copies of their digital photos or other personal files, which were never backed up.

But your files aren't the only thing of worth. The computing device itself has value—and not just in selling it.

Another class of malware causes your device to act as part of a botnet, which can be hundreds of thousands to millions of computing devices acting together. Two common uses of botnets are to attack websites and send out spam (usually through compromised email accounts).

Which brings us to the third target scope: your contacts.

There are botnets that scour the internet for email addresses. However, many of those emails may be invalid or generic, where they aren't directed to a specific person, such as webmaster@website.com.

If a hacker can access contact lists of known and valid emails, he now has a list he can spam, or sell to spammers. Those on the list can be targeted with plain old spam email or with more targeted phishing emails, which try to get you to give out personal information or login credentials.

More sophisticated criminals scour these lists for personal contact information of higher profile individuals. You may not be an executive officer, but maybe you know someone who is or who works closely with one.

But contacts aren't limited to email lists. Social media is a treasure trove of contact and personal information. In the wrong hands, and especially if your social media is public, your information can be used in social engineering attacks against you or others.

Many people have been scammed by someone pretending to be a family member in trouble. These scammers might contact a grandparent through social media and pretend to be a grandchild in a desperate situation, needing immediate assistance. Wanting to be helpful, and trusting the person is who they say they are, the grandparent (or other victim) acts in good faith, without independently verifying the truth.

Social engineering is just one type of identity theft.

Simply put, identity theft occurs when someone else pretends to be someone they are not. These fraudulent acts happen in the real world and virtually. Social Security numbers can be used to open accounts. Compromised credentials are used to log in to computing systems.

Unauthorized transactions occur with stolen credit card information. These are all cases where someone's identity is used fraudulently.

While most of the time identity theft causes financial problems, I once had a student share his unusual story. He discovered his Social Security number had been used to open some accounts. As the investigation continued, he learned that the person who stole his identity was an illegal alien who had used the Social Security number to get a job and open an account. Unusual activity was what initially alerted him, and by examining the credit history and performing some investigative work, he discovered the accounts. In an unusual twist, he learned that this illegal's actions had actually improved his credit score.

Unfortunately, the vast majority of identity theft cases are damaging to the victim. Most identify theft is for illegal and fraudulent purposes. Even though my student's credit score had improved, more of his personal information was being exposed to the illegal who had his Social Security number, and the exposure was beginning to negatively affect his online identity.

Even though the person who stole my student's identity was apparently good at managing credit, the Social Security number was being used illegally. As the victim, my student began a long process of separating his accounts from the illegally created ones.

I've known others who have the more typical experience. Their information was used to open a fraudulent account, their credit score takes a nose dive, and they are suddenly severely limited in what they can do financially—not to mention they face the daunting, lengthy process of clearing up the mess.

And it's not just adults who have identify theft problems. Children's Social Security numbers being used in identity theft is increasingly common. Unfortunately, these instances often don't come to light until years later, when the child has grown and wants to open an account only to discover his or her Social Security number has been used, misused, and abused.

So, you may not have millions of dollars. You may not be the executive of a Fortune 500 company. You may not be a high-profile community leader. But . . .

You are a target, and you need to protect yourself.

And, you need to help protect others. This isn't just being a good neighbor. If they protect their information, then it will, by association, help keep your information safer.

Best practices

"Best practices" are those procedures shown to be, or accepted as being, the most effective and that produce optimal results. Because best practices are expected to increase effectiveness and efficiency, they often become the standard. When it comes to security, best practices are considered the ideal methods to maximize protection of information systems.

Like most industries, there are a lot of best practices in information technology. When it comes to keeping your devices and information protected, four best practices are frequently advocated:

- Keep systems and applications up-to-date.
- Maintain an up-to-date antivirus (anti-malware) and perform regular scans.
- Regularly back up your data.
- Use secure passwords.

We'll take a look into each of these practices.

Updates—OS and applications

Keeping the operating system and applications up-to-date is among the most critical but unimplemented practice to maximize protection. Consider this: a hacker will generally try to steal your information by one of two general methods.

The easiest method is to ask you to hand over your account information or credentials. Most often, this is done through various forms of scams, phishing attacks, and malicious websites or links. The objective is to fool you into giving them the requested information through means that look deceptively legitimate.

The other method is to infect your device using some form of malware. The malware then does the work of trying to steal your information and passing it on to the hacker.

The malware takes advantage of two general types of vulnerabilities on your device: known or unknown. That's a bit of an oversimplification, but here's a little more detail.

A "known" vulnerability is a bug, flaw, or weakness that the system developer knows about. If the software or system is still in active production—meaning it's still being sold—then the company should be fixing problems as they are discovered. The fixes to the problems are often referred to as patches (just as you might patch a leak) or a security update. Sometimes a feature or other update will include security patches.

Over time, most software will have a lot of problems discovered. If the software isn't kept up-to-date, the original version will eventually have a lot of holes in it.

As other software is added to your computer (or other device), compatibility issues may cause vulnerabilities. Popular software applications should receive regular updates. It's not unheard of to have an operating system update and then for an application developer to issue an update soon after.

After a time, the programming code for an operating system, or other software, becomes too impractical to maintain, or new coding methods are developed that make a new version more efficient and effective. When that happens, the developer may have an "end of life" period for the old version of the operating system or software. During that time, the company will likely continue to fix problems, but new features won't be worked on.

When the system or software reaches its end of life, the company will stop creating new patches. But, that doesn't mean security problems will stop being exposed. The reality is, more security holes will be discovered, and, since no patches will be made, the system will become increasingly vulnerable.

Those who continue to use out-of-date software—whether they have chosen not to install the patches or they are using software that is no longer being patched—risk having a vulnerability exploited.

If malware tries to exploit an already-patched vulnerability on your computer, then the malware is basically harmless on that machine. However, if a patch was issued, but the user (including a system administrator or company) chooses not to install the patch or update, then the malware can still take advantage of the vulnerability.

There have been a lot of data breaches that could have been prevented had the systems been patched first. Just like non-IT people, system administrators will put off updating or patching systems for a variety of reasons: it's too complicated, it might affect how applications are running, they're too busy, or they procrastinate because of laziness.

The "unknown" vulnerabilities are generally referred to as zero-day vulnerabilities. The name comes from the fact that the developer doesn't know about the vulnerability and has had "zero" days to create a patch for the system.

Antivirus

Next to keeping your operating system updated, you need an updated anti-malware (antivirus) program on your system.

There is a false perception that Apple computers are somehow immune to malware or don't get infected. Here's the reality.

When computers began to be popular, Microsoft's operating system dominated the market. Most businesses using computers had systems running the Microsoft Windows operating system.

The cybercriminals, just like most criminals, focused on money and the bigger target, which was the Windows-based operating systems.

Another component to the PC-Apple-Malware debate is that Microsoft plays nicer with third party developers. That's why there is more software and hardware available for Windows-based computers. Apple is much more tight-fisted with allowing others to play in the Mac OS system. As a result, fewer software and hardware players exist in the Mac world.

Because there are so many more software and hardware developers for Windows-based computers, there are also that many more potential problems and vulnerabilities that may be discovered and exploited. The infamous blue-screen-of-death, where the Windows computer freezes up and may restart, is often caused by third party issues.

Combine the higher potential for vulnerabilities with the much higher number of users in the PC environment, and it makes sense that hackers would put a greater effort in developing malware for Windows than Mac.

What I've noticed is that Microsoft has become much more adept, and forthcoming, about security issues and issuing patches. I haven't noticed as much openness from Apple, where it sometimes seems vulnerabilities are ignored or silently patched. If you are under the preconception that Macs are more secure, don't get complacent; there are serious Mac OS–specific vulnerabilities and malware on the web, so do not believe an Apple machine is immune.

Here's the advantage and problem. The Mac OS is generally immune to malware that exploits Windows vulnerabilities. Similarly, Windows computers are basically immune to Mac OS malware. The problem is, Mac computers may end up sharing malware with a Windows machine, and Windows computers might pass a Mac infection on to an Apple device.

The bottom line is both Mac and PC computers need updated anti-malware on them.

Having up-to-date anti-malware can also help protect you from old malware. Remember how an unpatched OS can be vulnerable to malware that exploits old vulnerabilities? Well, an updated anti-malware might catch the infection before it causes problems. The key word is "might." It's much better if both the system and anti-malware are kept updated.

The anti-malware should perform regular scans of the system and storage devices. You should also run an occasional manual scan, choosing a deep scan option, if available.

Backups

Reality check: your data is not secure until you have reliable backups in place. Note the plural "s" at the end of backup.

A single backup is better than none, but at least two copies provide some redundancy. I prefer one backup to be on a removable storage device and the second copy to be on a cloud storage.

What's the "cloud?"

The "cloud" is anything not local to your computing device. Normally it is a service somewhere on the internet. Since we don't usually know where the service is hosted, it's a nebulous idea and someone, somewhere, decided "cloud" was a good description.

A common cloud-based service is cloud storage, like Dropbox, Google Drive, OneDrive, iCloud and dozens of other cloud-storage providers.

A cloud-based backup is convenient for a couple reasons:

- You don't have to provide a physical storage device.
- You can access it anywhere you have internet.

Beyond a trial, or limited free options, there is usually a regular subscription fee associated with cloud accounts. When considering cloud storage, there are a few limitations to keep in mind:

- You have to trust the cloud service provider to keep your data secure.
- You will need internet access to get to your backup.
- If you have a large number of files, restoring your backed-up files may take a long time.

Another potential limitation to be aware of concerning cloud storage is that while most malicious software attacks files on the computer—looking for the common "C" drive—there are some malware variants that search for any storage device connected to the computer. This can include folder locations, such as connected drives.

As an added measure of security, it's a good idea to regularly back up your files to a storage device that is normally disconnected from the computer. For example, you temporarily connect a portable hard drive, copy your files to it, and then disconnect the drive.

Secure passwords

Passwords will be discussed in greater detail in Chapter 3. For now, where passwords are concerned, there are two general best practices.

First, don't use the same password for all your accounts.

Second, your passwords should be secure. By secure, I mean your password should be long and use a variety of characters so it's also complex. Short passwords, especially those that use a limited character set, are easily cracked.

In Chapter 3, we'll cover how to make your passwords long and complex, while still being memorable, and how you can easily maintain a long list of secure passwords.

CHAPTER 2

Computers 101

Before we start talking about computer security, it may be helpful to establish a common base. At times I may refer to certain parts of a computer, such as memory, storage, or processor. A basic understanding of computer parts, as well as other computer and network-related terms, can be helpful. Don't worry—I'll try to keep it simple because you don't really need to know how things work, just have the idea of their job functions.

If you're already familiar with the workings of computers, networking, and their associated components, you're probably good to skip this chapter. But, you may find it helpful when trying to explain things to non-technical users.

We'll begin by comparing the computer to a typical office, where there's a desk, file cabinet, and person doing the work.

When a computer is powered on, it's like the light being turned on in the office so the person can get to work.

The person is the main part of the office and performs most of the work.

Files are retrieved from the file cabinet and taken to the desk. The papers from a file can be opened on the desk and used fairly efficiently. Multiple files can also be retrieved and used. However, as more files get piled on the desk, things become a little more confusing and less efficient as the worker moves between different files.

Having multiple files on the desk can become even more burdensome if our desk is small, so a simple solution is to get a bigger desk. A bigger desk allows for more files to be used efficiently.

With a small desk, we either need to put files back into the file drawer and take them out when needed, or we end up stacking the files and shuffling through them to find what is needed.

How does this compare to a computer? On a computer, the file cabinet is the computer's storage. Most computers have a hard drive as the main storage. Our programs and data files are stored on the hard drive, and, just like a file cabinet, the hard drive is formatted into an indexing system so programs and files can be easily found, retrieved, and opened.

The desk is like the computer's memory, or RAM (random access memory). The memory is where the work is performed; it's the workspace. Like a large desk, a large amount of memory will help your computer run faster because the processor can work on the files much more efficiently, without having to either flip through files or bring files in and out of storage.

On the other hand, a small amount of memory is the equivalent of a small desk. The computer doesn't run as efficiently, and multiple programs and opened files start to bog down the computer.

The person at the desk is like the computer's processor, or CPU (central processing unit). When an application is launched, or a file is retrieved, the processor goes to the storage, finds the application or file, and brings it to the memory. With the file in memory, the processor can perform calculations and other work as needed with the file.

The processor, memory, and storage are key components of a computing system, although there are other parts as well.

A computer usually has a display attached. With many machines, part of the memory is allocated to showing images on the display. It's the equivalent of part of the desk being used up before you even open a program. Some computers will have a video card, or dedicated video memory. This is like an extension to your desk devoted to the video display, so all the regular memory is available for other needs.

There is a difference between memory and storage. Storage is non-volatile, where memory is volatile. This doesn't mean it's going to go explode. It refers to the stability of the information stored.

Volatile storage (the memory or RAM) can only store information when the computer is on, when the memory has power.

The hard drive, as non-volatile storage, will continue to keep files stored, even without power.

There are two general types of hard drives: one is traditional magnetic-based hard disk drives (HDD) and the other is flash-memory–based solid-state drives (SSD). For our discussion, a "hard drive" could be any type of long-term storage.

When you shut down the computer, anything stored in the memory is gone. This is why you need to save files you're working on. Saving a file stores a copy on the hard drive. Newer applications have gotten better about auto-saving, or at least saving a temporary file, just in case something happens and you forgot to save.

There is a difference between shutting down a computer and putting it to sleep. Before most shutdown processes, files need to be saved; otherwise the computer will probably ask you to save them before it will proceed with the shutdown. The shutdown process will close all programs, applications, and processes. Virtually no power is used after a computer has been shut down (a very small amount of electricity will continue to be used, if the computer is plugged in).

Sleep will essentially suspend the applications and programs that were running when the computer was put to sleep. Power will be used, although at a much lower rate, as the computer will need to keep power to the memory. When the computer is powered on, it will more rapidly return to its previous working state.

Hardware, software, firmware—what is -ware?

Computer hardware basically consists of anything attached to the computer that you can touch. All the electronics inside the computer are part of the hardware as well as the connected accessories (display, printer, keyboard, mouse, etc.). Generally speaking, computer accessories attached to the computer are called peripherals.

Software is the programming code that runs operating systems, programs, applications, etc. Software contains the instructions for the computer to perform certain tasks. Software code is written in a variety of different programming languages, and those languages vary from low-level machine assembly language to higher-level code that nearly resembles our language. Software is stored on the hard drive, and when the operating system launches an application, the code is brought into the computer's memory. If a program is running and the computer loses power, the running program is lost. The code is still on the hard drive, so the program should be able to run again. However, occasionally an abrupt power outage can cause an error to be introduced into the code, causing some corruption. This is why when a computer is shut down, the applications are all closed first.

Firmware is a special type of software that is stored on special chips in the hardware. Unlike software, if the power goes out, firmware does not normally get erased.

On most computers, when the computer is powered on, the firmware starts up and begins detecting the various hardware attached. It may also launch the operating system.

As the operating system starts up, it launches a variety of sub-programs referred to as processes. It also loads drivers, which are pieces of software that tell the operating system how to use certain hardware.

The many types of software on a computer may run at different levels, which may allow access to differing parts of the system and hardware. Many of the main processes of the operating system run at a "root" level. The root level controls and manages all of the code running at upper layers and has what might be called master control access to all parts of the computer. User accounts that have administrator rights have access to the root level. Most computer infections attempt to gain administrator access to the machine.

What is the "C" drive?

Back when personal computers began to make their mark, there wasn't a hard drive. Programs were loaded into the memory from a floppy drive. Most computers designated the first floppy drive as the "A" drive, and some had a second floppy drive, the "B" drive.

When hard drives came around, they were designated the "C" drive, mostly because computers still had at least an "A" drive.

Computers will also boot, start up, in a designated order. Older computers would start with the "A" drive, move to the "B", and then run the "C" drive if nothing was bootable from the earlier drives. Originally the hardware was configured to create the boot order. Now the order is easily arranged in the firmware settings.

Hard drive types

As previously mentioned, the hard drive is the main storage location for applications and data on your computer.

Traditional magnetic hard disk drives (HDD) have a spinning metal platter (usually more than one), with magnetic spindles that glide barely across the surfaces of the disks. Although HDDs have become more resistant to adverse forces (such as bumps and drops), they still use moving parts.

Solid-state drives (SSD) use flash memory instead of magnetic disks to store information.

Flash memory is electronic storage. Unlike RAM, flash memory does not require constant electricity to maintain the data. If the power goes off, data stored on flash memory is still there. Flash memory is what thumb drives (flash drives) use, so an SSD is comparable to a large-capacity flash drive.

SSDs are typically much faster, use less power, and are more robust than HDDs. However, they cost more per gigabyte and don't (yet) come in capacities as large as HDDs.

Some computers will use an SSD for the operating system and applications, so programs will launch and run faster, and also have a larger HDD for storing files.

However, many computer manufacturers expect users to use cloud-based storage for excessive files, so they don't see as much of an issue with SSDs that are smaller than HDDs.

Portable & external drives

The hard drive in the computer is an internal hard drive. Drives used outside of the computer, often plugged in to a USB port, are external or portable drives. External drives typically use a USB connection to the computer and have a power adapter plugged in to them. External drives are normally left in place because they aren't as convenient to move with the additional power cable.

Portable hard drives simply plug in to a USB port. They receive the power they need through the USB connection. Portable drives are designed to be convenient to transport, especially since they don't require an additional power source.

Gigabytes and terabytes

Data on a digital device is stored and transmitted in a binary format. It starts with the bit (identified by a lowercase "b"), which is either a 1 or 0. While programming languages are written in a human-friendly format, the code is eventually translated (compiled) into a machine-readable format. These bits of binary are classified into larger designations.

Eight bits of data make a byte (identified by the uppercase "B"). Following a binary format, bytes are doubled from 8 to 16, 32, 64, 128, 256, 516, 1024, and so on.

If you have 1,024 bytes, it's called a kilobyte (KB). From there, 1,024 kilobytes—or 1,024,000 bytes—is one megabyte (MB).

Giga refers to billions, so 1 gigabyte (GB) is 1,024 megabytes, or 1,024,000,000 bytes.

After a gigabyte, we move to the terabyte (TB); 1 terabyte is 1,024 gigabytes.

In the consumer sphere, we haven't reached the next levels yet, but after terabyte comes petabyte, exabyte, zettabyte, and yottabyte.

When referring to larger numbers in computers, we need to keep in mind that computers work in binary. These large numbers are in powers of 1,024 instead of our normal powers of 1,000. But, for simplicity, we often round the numbers. So, while 1,024,000 bytes equals 1 megabyte, we'll usually just think of 1 MB as being 1,000,000 bytes.

This is also the reason for the discrepancy as to why your portable drive says it's a certain size, but when you plug it in, the computer recognizes it as less. We'll use a small 4 GB flash drive as an example. The manufacturer claims it has 4 GB of space, but when you plug it in to the computer, only about 3.7 GB appear. Did the manufacturer lie?

Nope. The manufacturer is marketing the size based on our common understanding of numbers, in the base 10 format. To find out how many bytes the computer sees, we need to divide the advertised number of bytes by 1,204 KB, then by 1,024 MB, and finally by 1,024 GB to discover how many gigabytes there actually are.

4,000,000,000 bytes / 1,204 KB = 3,906,250 KB

3,906,250 KB / 1,024 MB = 3,814.697 MB

3,814.69 MB / 1,024 GB = 3.725 GB

Because of this discrepancy, there are special binary prefixes that refer to the powers of 1,024. These prefixes are kibi, mebi, gibi, tebi, and pedi. Basically, the binary prefix takes the first two letters of the regular prefix and then adds "bi" to them. However, I haven't seen these prefixes used in the IT field, and I doubt many IT personnel are aware of them.

Networking

Networking allows our multitude of devices to communicate to each other from within our local area network and to other locations outside of our local network.

The local area network (LAN) consists of all the devices and components within a connected environment, such as a business or home.

From the LAN's perspective, the internet consists of the devices, websites, and other network locations external to the local network.

For a device to connect to other devices within a LAN, they generally need to have a network adapter (wireless or Ethernet) and a network switch that the devices are connected to. To communicate outside of the network, they go through a router that acts as a gateway to the internet.

Devices connecting over the network cables are using Ethernet communication protocols, so often the wired network connection is referred to as Ethernet.

There are several communication protocols wireless devices use, but most of the time it's just called Wi-Fi.

Routers

When the internet connection enters your home (or office), its first stop is usually a router (in some connections, like from a phone company or cable provider, there may be a modem either before or as part of the router). The router, which may also act as a network switch, connects to the devices within the LAN.

The router routes network traffic. For devices trying to connect to a website, or location outside of the local network, the router receives the request and sends it out to the web.

When the response to a web request is received, the router is the first stop for the web traffic coming into the local network. The router looks at the web response to find out which device it's meant for and routes the traffic to the right device.

Because the router sends web traffic to the internet, and receives and routes traffic within the local network, it's often referred to as a gateway.

Switches

A network switch provides some functionality similar to a router in that it can send network traffic to specified locations within the local network. However, a switch cannot send or receive network traffic to or from the internet.

For the wired network, Ethernet cables connect computers to the switch or router.

In a wireless network, a Wi-Fi switch, called an access point, is used to connect devices to the local network.

Most consumer Wi-Fi routers combine the functionality of a network switch (where you can plug devices into the router) and a wireless access point. The router is the gateway for the Ethernet and Wi-Fi devices to connect to the internet.

Network adapters

Also known as network controllers or network interface cards (NIC), network adaptors can be Ethernet or wireless controllers. The network adapter is how the computer connects to the network. Most computers have an Ethernet connection built in, and laptops and mobile devices have built-in wireless adapters.

Addressing

Computer networking is based on an addressing system. Most computer addresses are referred to as an "IP address." "IP" refers to "internet protocol," which is the communication protocol most network-connected devices use. Whole books are dedicated to networking, so this will be an over-simplification of networking.

Where IP addressing is concerned, there are public and private addresses. The IP addresses used to access websites on the internet are public addresses. In most home and business networks, the devices within the LAN have private IP addresses assigned to them while they are in the LAN.

Public IP addresses, or a range (block) of addresses, are purchased. Many larger organizations have purchased public IP addresses, but most individuals and small businesses have not. Because a public IP address is used to access the internet, so most individuals and businesses rely on an Internet Service Provider.

Internet Service Providers (ISPs) have blocks of IP addresses which they *lease* out to their customers. When the routers of their customers contact the ISP, requesting internet access, the router is assigned an IP address. This leased IP address, usually a public IP, is the gateway address for the local network to connect to the internet. So, for most people, access to the internet goes through the ISP.

When your device connects to a network, it sends out a message saying it wants to connect. In most cases, a system (usually a server, but it can also be a router) uses DHCP (Dynamic Host Configuration Protocol) to respond to the address request and assigns an IP address to the adapter on the device. The device then uses the information provided by the DHCP server to configure its network connection. In most local networks, the IP address assigned to the device is private IP.

When it's time to go to a website on the internet, the device sends the web request out to the router/gateway, and the gateway will send the request to a Domain Name Server/System (DNS). The DNS is like a big address book that matches website names (which are what we are familiar with) to the corresponding IP address. From there, the web request can be forwarded (routed) to the right destination.

We can compare this to sending a letter to Joe Public. Unlike people, where multiple people might have the same name, online website names (and public IP addresses) are unique and registered. The web address is referred to as a URL (Uniform Resource Locator). Combining the information in the DNS and URL, the letter is forwarded through various routers across the internet to the IP address where the URL is located.

In our example, the DNS tells us that Joe Public lives on 3100 West 8000 South in Cyber City. The mail then gets routed to Joe Public's address.

Similarly, when we type in a web address, the DNS resolves the address (finds the corresponding IP address), and our web request is sent to the right place.

That is for public IP addresses. But it works a little differently for private IP addresses, which are what the devices in most home and business networks are assigned while they are in the LAN.

A private address could be compared to an apartment complex or even post office boxes. The apartment complex, or post office box, has a physical street address, which would be like the public IP address. However, in private addressing, the individual PO box numbers, or apartment numbers, are not used when making external requests. Part of the reason private IPs are not used externally is there may be thousands of private networks using the same private addresses.

Let's say John Private lives in an apartment complex with 50 others. While inside the apartment network, he and the other tenants can easily communicate with each other by using their apartment numbers. But, to communicate outside of their local network, their communications are routed through a gateway. All external communications are given the public address of the apartment building, along with some additional routing information pertaining to which apartment the communication came from.

For John Private to contact Joe Public, John first sends a request to Joe Public. The apartment router receives Private's message, affixes some additional routing information to it, then sends it to the DNS, where it gets forwarded to Joe Public's address.

Joe Public then responds, and the response is routed back to the public address of the apartments. At that point, the router looks for additional routing information, sees that it came from John, and forwards it to John Private's apartment.

However, if Mark Maul tries to send unwanted messages to John Private, he sends them to the public address of the apartments. But, since he doesn't have the private routing information, the apartment router doesn't know where to forward the message and discards it. However, if John initiated the contact Mr. Maul would have the routing information to send information back to Private's apartment.

Speed

When we connect our devices to the local network and the internet, we want fast connections. Network speed is usually identified by megabit or gigabit connections. Mega- or gigabit speed is referenced in bits per second (bps). Most high-speed internet service providers (ISPs) measure their speeds in gigabits per second (Gbps). Slower networks are still measured in megabits per second (Mbps).

A similar discrepancy to hard drive size versus actual size is experienced in network speeds. The first thing to note is if the speed is in bits or bytes. A 1 gigabyte (GB) connection is 8 gigabits. But, most of the time a gig speed network is a 1 gigabit per second (Gbps) connection, which is one-eighth as fast as a 1 GBps connection. Basically, it's marketing where "giga" is more impressive sounding than "mega."

Remember, the internet service provider gives you the speed in our normal base ten number and not the binary version. Here's the reality of a 1 Gbps connection:

    1,000,000,000 bits = 125,000,000 bytes (or 125 MB)

    125,000,000 bytes / 1024 kb = 122,070.3125 KB

    122,070.3125 KB / 1,024 MB = 119.209 MB

So, what you thought might have been confused with a 1 giga*byte* connection, is actually only a 119 MB connection. But, the actual speed will probably be slower due to other network factors. So, if your 1 gigabit network is getting 80 to 100 megabytes per second, it's actually doing well. Still, it's a lot faster than megabit connections.

If you have a gigabit network connection in your home, you should make sure all the network components in your home match or exceed the speed from the ISP. If a piece of your home network can't handle the speed from the ISP, it will act as a bottleneck and slow network traffic down.

The speed capability of older network devices is usually rated as 10/100 megabit. Newer components should be 10/100/1000 megabit (Mb), which are gigabit capable.

We've already mentioned the two general ways devices connect to network—either through a wired (Ethernet) connection or through a wireless (Wi-Fi) connection.

Wireless is more convenient, but it may be more susceptible to interference. Ethernet connections are usually more reliable and faster than Wi-Fi.

Bandwidth

Bandwidth is how much data can flow through the network. Think of the network like a highway. The network highway may be capable of 120-megabyte speed, but if there's a lot of network traffic, the speed is affected, just like more cars on the road at rush hour slow speeds well below the posted limit.

If one of your network components can't handle the speed limit, even if there isn't any other traffic, it'll be like your devices are trying to speed past a forced speed reduction. Overall traffic won't pass the bottleneck any faster than the limitation will allow, so the limitation affects the flow of the entire network.

VPN

A VPN, or virtual private network, allows you to connect your device to a specific network over the internet. Using a VPN application, you connect to the network, using your login credentials, and your device becomes a virtual part of that network. Think of the connection being like a tunnel that protects the communication between your device and the network from outside influences.

When you are on a public Wi-Fi network, one way to increase security for your device is to use a VPN to connect to a secure network. The VPN establishes a protected connection between you and the secure network, and from that network, you can more safely access the internet.

Firewall

A physical firewall is a partition or wall that is designed to prevent or inhibit the spread of fire. Firewalls are found in many buildings and vehicles. In a vehicle, the firewall separates the engine compartment from the cabin, where the driver and passengers are. Most firewalls have secure openings to allow wires, pipes, or other objects to pass safely through.

In computing, firewalls are similar. Firewalls can be software- or hardware-based and on a computer or on the network. In any case, the objective of the firewall is to keep harmful stuff (the fire) out, protect what is inside, and only allow permitted applications, processes, or ports through.

Opening a port, or allowing an application, through the firewall is akin to an authorized wire or pipe running through the building or vehicle firewall. If unneeded ports are open in a firewall, it's like cutting holes in a real firewall, compromising the safety of the occupants by making it easier for fire to pass through.

Just like a firewall doesn't prevent all fires and doesn't stop other harmful things from damaging the building or vehicle, a computer firewall does not stop your device (or network) from getting malware. But, it is a valuable defense against malicious acts. And, having unneeded ports open, or even disabling the firewall, puts your system at increased risk.

Lifespan of hardware

Sometimes I get asked about how long a piece of hardware should last. This isn't directly applicable to how computers or networks work, but it's an important consideration that should be addressed. And, it is applicable to maintaining the security of your digital information.

In my experience, most hardware should give at least three years of good, reliable use. Much of the time hardware may easily last five years or more, depending on how it's used. Misuse, abuse, and abnormal overuse will certainly decrease its service life.

Business class hardware usually costs more than consumer grade, but it'll often handle a little more abuse and it's designed to tolerate greater use. That said, there's a reason it's rare to find a warranty lasting more than three years.

The most common hardware failures, or performance reductions, I've encountered occur with batteries and, sometimes, hard drives around the three-year mark. This is not saying they all fail. Most just really start having performance issues by this time. Failures are not common at this point, but the device, and especially the battery, will be experiencing a significant reduction in performance by the three-year mark.

Once a device reaches five years, I tell users it's living on borrowed time. The hardware could certainly last several more years, but it is reaching the end of its usability and reliability. If you have data relying on old hardware, you are risking increasing chances of data loss.

When someone asks me about whether they should get a new computer or not, one of the questions I usually ask is the age of their current machine. If the computer is less than three years old, its performance can usually be improved through various means as well as increasing its memory.

From three to five years, replacing the device is more at the discretion of the user. Performance can usually be improved, especially if the memory is increased and if system is wiped, and everything installed fresh. However, the reliability of the system is becoming questionable by this time.

After five years, the computer may still be perfectly good for kids to use, but a new computer is definitely preferable. When a computer gets to seven years, it will often have less capabilities than the low-end consumer models you can get for a couple hundred dollars, or less.

Cryptocurrency

In the computer and technology industry, cryptocurrency is a relatively new area that is receiving a lot of attention. While not directly related to your computer's hardware or software, cryptocurrency is something you should be aware of because there will be increasing moves towards technologies that support cryptocurrency.

Cryptocurrency is digital, or virtual, currency. Most likely you've heard of BitCoin, which is the most familiar cryptocurrency. Other cryptocurrencies in use include Litecoin, Namecoin, and Ethereum, among many others. The aggregate market value of cryptocurrencies is estimated to be over $120 billion, with BitCoin representing about 50 percent of the total value.[1]

The allure of cryptocurrency is the security, ease, and reduced cost of transactions. A trusted third party, such as a bank or credit card company, isn't needed. The security keys of the transaction are in the user's account. Many institutions see believe cryptocurrency will not only lower transaction costs but also make payments more efficient and nearly immediate.

Most cryptocurrencies use a technology called blockchain. Blockchain uses a distributed ledger where all online transactions ever conducted are stored in virtual ledgers and copied across all computers running the technology. Each new transaction block is verified by the ledgers of the other users of the technology. As a result, it's almost impossible to forge transaction histories.

If it hasn't already, it's likely cryptocurrency may take a role in your financial future. Because increasing your security and privacy is what this book's about, this is a heads up. A basic understanding of cryptocurrency is also helpful when we later discuss a fairly new form of malware called cryptojacking.

CHAPTER 3

Passwords and Authentication

Now that we've established that you are a target and we've gone over some computer and network basics, it's time for what has become a critical part of cybersecurity: passwords. While passwords may not be the most important security factor, they are like the key to a locked door. For most accounts, your password is the key to entry.

Simple passwords are simple keys on a simple lock—easy to pick and open.

Long and complex passwords make that lock much more complicated to crack open.

Of course, there's more to it, but that's the simplified explanation.

Before we dive in to passwords, we should cover some key points to security, which apply to passwords.

The three main pillars in cybersecurity are confidentiality, integrity, and availability. Most security books identify these as the CIA triad. However, some sources refer to the triad as AIC so it's not confused with the Central Intelligence Agency. As we briefly cover these three principles, keep in mind that services or systems could be substituted for "data."

Confidentiality means data should only be seen by those who have been given access to it. Another security principle called "least privilege" applies, which means users should not be given more access than needed to perform their job. Confidentiality is supported by correct identification, authentication, and authorization of users. More simply, this principle is ensuring the right person has access to the right system. The combination of a username and password are the common key to identifying and authenticating users and granting them access to the systems they are authorized to use.

Integrity is the principle that data is protected from unauthorized change. This applies to data that is stored or transferred across a network. Combining this with confidentiality, we want to make sure the right person, given the right credentials, can access the right data on the right system.

Availability is the principle that data is accessible when it is needed. Adding to the other two principles, it is the right person, accessing the right data, on the right system, at the right time.[2]

In other words, the credentials you use to log in to a system determine whether you're allowed in, what you have access to, and what you can, or can't, do in the system.

Passwords play an important role in keeping your information confidential. Only the person who enters valid credentials (such as a username and password) should be authorized to access the confidential information. Properly authenticated users should also be the only ones with permissions to modify, add to, or delete the data.

The challenge we face is, every site where we create an account needs a username and password. After a short time, you might have dozens of accounts.

Usernames are fairly easy to create and remember, as most sites accept an email address for the username.

For simplicity and ease (and laziness) most people tend to use the same password for most (or every) online account.

So, what happens if hackers manage to get your username and password?

They might try those credentials to log in to your email account. If successful, what might they find? Maybe a bunch of email from the other accounts you have. Notices of bank statements. Maybe a privacy notice from your credit card company. How about email from other institutions and organizations, many of which you may have an online account with.

Now the hackers have a list of websites to try your username (email address) and password on.

If you simply used the same password on all those sites, you have now opened your doors wide to the hackers, essentially giving them free access to your personal information.

Because secure passwords, and their protection, are so foundational to good cybersecurity, this chapter will be longer than others.

Old to new guidelines

Back in 2003, the National Institute of Standards and Technology (NIST) published a document with recommendations for password security. Bill Burr, the NIST manager who wrote the document, advised password complexity, which included the use of special characters, capital letters, and numbers. Among the guidelines were recommendations for regular password changes—such as those requiring you to change your password every 90 days. To meet the "best practice" of complexity, organizations began requiring specified mixes of lowercase and uppercase letters, numbers, and special characters. Most sites required a minimum length of six to eight characters. And many sites began implementing regular password change requirements.

However, analyses of breached password databases have shown the rules were not as significant to password security as expected. Instead, the rules affected usability and memorability, and, as an unintended consequence, actually reduced password security. Many users, when faced with frequent password changes, would simply make a small change, like adding or changing a number, or they would write down their passwords. I have seen many passwords written down as I've helped users over the years. The complexity requirements and frequent password changes makes passwords easy to forget.

NIST made significant changes in their password recommendations in 2017. Complexity is still a factor, but the biggest change is in length, with the guidelines recommending users be able to use long passphrases. While the recommendation is still a minimum of eight characters, NIST suggests allowing up to 64 characters for passwords. The new guidelines are against password hints and user questions (like "what's your mother's maiden name?") which could be seen, or guessed, by others.

The new guidelines also recommend comparing passwords against a blacklist of weak or commonly used passwords, dictionary words, sequential characters, or the name of the service or username. Additionally, the guidelines recommend not requiring password changes, unless there's evidence of a compromised password.

Some of the other factors in the new guidelines include the use of multi-factor authentication, device identification, web browser authentication, threats and security considerations, mitigation strategies, privacy considerations, and biometric usability.

Let's go a bit more in depth into creating a strong password/passphrase.

Password strength

Determining the strength of a password is a little complicated. What you do need to know is the strength of a password is based on two factors: length and complexity.

Strength in length

The length of a password is where the greatest strength (and security) lies. Length is simply how many characters are in the password.

The shorter the password, the easier (and quicker) it is to crack. Cracking means discovering what the actual password is. Security-conscious organizations will never store passwords in what is known as plain-text, which is human readable. Instead, passwords should be stored in an encrypted format. More on that in a little bit.

Conversely, longer passwords are harder to crack. For a long time, complexity was considered more important, but in the last few years there has been a shift. Complexity is still important, but length is seen as a bigger determinant in password strength.

Complexity

Complexity of a password is how many different character sets are included in the passwords. Really simple passwords use only numbers, as there are only 10 unique digits. A program used for cracking passwords would only need to go through all numbers until it finds a match. And computers can do that fairly quickly.

A password using only lowercase letters in the English alphabet has a complexity of 26 characters. This is considerably more complex that using only numbers.

Likewise, a password utilizing only uppercase letters also has only 26 characters.

However, if the password has a mix of uppercase and lowercase letters, the complexity level has gone from 26 to 52. Add the 10 digits and complexity increases to 62.

But, what about special characters?

Some systems limit which special characters are allowed. Maybe only 8 special characters (!, @, #, $, &, *, -, and _) are permitted. That would still increase the complexity to 70.

If all punctuation and special characters on a typical US keyboard are allowed, 33 characters are added to the complexity.

Combined, these 95 characters are the printable ASCII character set. ASCII, or the American Standard Code for Information Interchange, is how a human-readable character is encoded so a machine knows what it is.

If characters from other languages are allowed, it further increases complexity. For now, we'll stick with the 95 characters.

Exponential power in complexity

Let's look at the power of complexity and length in creating a strong, secure password. To find the power, we will employ exponents, taking our complexity number and raising it to an exponential power.

First, we'll look at using the 10 digits. The complexity number is the base, which, in this case, is 10. The length of the password is the power number. If our password is only four digits long, then we have 10 to the power of 4, or 10^4. Factoring this out (10 x 10 x 10 x 10), there are 10,000 possible number combinations.

A password cracker wouldn't even break a sweat with only 10,000 possibilities. It would probably seem like it was just waiting for you to press enter because it will almost immediately return the cracked password.

Now let's add the lowercase letters and keep a four-character password. The number of possible combinations is now 36^4 (the 36 is from 10 numbers plus 26 lowercase letters, the 4 is the length of the password) or 1,679,616.

Double the length of the password to eight and we get 36^8, or 2,821,109,907,456 (that's almost three trillion) possible combinations.

Double the length again to 16 characters long (so it's 36^{16}), and the number of possible combinations increases to (numbers are rounded) 7,958,661,109,946,400,884,391,936.

Now add uppercase characters to the mix, and we'll start back with a four-character password.

With a base of 62 (52 letters and 10 numbers) and the power of 4 (62^4), the number of possible combinations is 14,776,336. That is more than eight times bigger than the number of combinations using lowercase letters and numbers.

Increase the password length to 16 characters, and the possible combinations jumps to 47,672,401,706,823,533,450,263,330,816.

If the full 95 printable characters of the ASCII set were allowed, a 16-character password would have the following number of possible combinations (95^{16}):

44,012,666,865,176,569,775,543,212,890,625

However, the full 95 characters aren't allowed on most password systems. So, let's just consider the possibility of using 70 characters: 52 for the letters, 10 numbers, and 8 special characters.

Unless the system you are on doesn't allow for it, I recommend passwords be at least 16 characters long. I prefer 20 characters or longer. Most of my passwords have been around the 20-character length because the system wouldn't accept anything longer.

Here's the difference between 16 characters long and 20 characters (these numbers are rounded).

$70^{16} = 3.32 \times 10^{29}$

$70^{20} = 7.98 \times 10^{36}$

Adding the four extra characters to the password increases the number of possibilities by more than 24 million.

While these numbers, and the calculations leading to them, may not be all that interesting to some people, hopefully you can at least begin to appreciate the importance of having a long password, and not just a complex one. In a later section, we'll show how quickly weaker passwords can be cracked.

The next question is, how do you make an easy-to-remember, long, and complex password?

Making passwords easy to remember

The buzzword is "passphrase." A password implies a single word or something short. "Passphrase" suggests something longer, but, hopefully, easier to remember.

The idea is to use a long phrase, or even sentence, as your "password." Let's go over a few of the suggestions to help you create a memorable passphrase.

One suggestion is to take the first letter of each word from a sentence to create your passphrase. For example, you might use a line from a poem. We'll use a well-known nursery rhyme:

> Mary had a little lamb, whose fleece was white as snow

Taking the first letters of each word, we get

> Mhallwfwwas

Without much effort, we created an 11-character password that uses both uppercase and lowercase letters.

We can increase complexity by adding numbers and special characters.

One common, easy-to-implement idea is to replace letters with a similar-looking number or special character.

Some commonly used replacements include:

Table 1: Common character substitutions.

For	You Might Use
A or a	@, h
H or h	4
S or s	&, $
O or o	0
E or e	3
I or i	1, !
L or l	1, 7
G or g	9

In addition to the replacements, another uppercase letter could be added. For this example, we'll change the "w" that represents "whose" to the capital letter.

So "Mhallwfwwas" would become "M4allWfww@$" or something similar.

Passwords are considered stronger if they do not start or end with a number. This is most because certain password crackers can be set to only use numbers in the place of beginning or ending characters.

Personally, I think length trumps number placement because unless the hacker knows how long your password is, it's hard to guess how many characters might be numbers.

For some people, a passphrase that takes the first letter of each word from a sentence is easy to remember. For me, not so much.

Using the same nursery rhyme, I'll just stick with the first phrase, "Mary had a little lamb."

Just as it is, the phrase is 22 characters long, with the spaces included. A lot of systems don't allow for spaces as a special character, so let's choose a special character to represent a space, such as a hyphen. To mix things up, we'll make the last letter a capital, and replace a few characters. With those changes, the passphrase becomes more memorable:

M@ry-h@d-a-7!ttle-7@mB

We now have a 22-character password that utilizes uppercase and lowercase letters, numbers, and special characters.

Now that we have a memorable password, the trick is to not use the same password for every account.

The best practice is to use a different password for each account, but most of us don't want to come up with something new for every site and then try to remember which site had which password.

Instead of having new passwords for every site, you might have five to seven different passwords. Not quite the "best practice," but it keeps your main accounts separate.

Use one password for your main email.

Have a second password for your primary financial institution.

A third password would be for your social media.

A fourth password for work.

The fifth password would be for other sites, those which require you to create an account but don't have any personal information other than your email address and name.

While this isn't the ideal, it's better than using the same password for all your sites. At least with this, if someone hacks your social media, they can't use the same password on your email or financial institution.

Another option is to create a personal passphrase pattern.

In the pattern, you could choose four parts. The first three parts will be the same for all passphrases. The fourth part changes for each site.

The first part is a word. You might use a name, a place, a hobby, or anything memorable. Maybe even a favorite object. For our example, let's use a holiday, Easter. Let's make a few changes, using uppercase and lowercase letters, a number, and a special character, so Easter becomes "East3R."

The second part of the pattern is a number. A four-digit year can be a memorable number. But, you might choose the last part of a phone number, street address, or zip code. For our example, we'll pick 2015.

It's better if the first two parts don't have any direct relationship, like using a name and birthyear. Keeping the two parts unrelated is a better idea. However, we're shooting for length as well as easy on the memory.

The third part is a character, or characters, you want to use as separators, or spaces. You might use one special character as the "space" between words and another before the number part. We'll keep it simple and just use the underscore character as our space.

These first and second parts, along with the spacing character(s) for the third part, should make up at least 12 characters of your password. In our example, by combining the name, number, and spacing parts, our passphrase begins with "E@st3R_2015_." All together these three parts give us 12 characters. The longer the password is the better, but my recommendation is a minimum total passphrase length of 16 characters, with a preferred minimum of 20 characters. So, 12 characters in the first three parts leaves us needing at least another four characters.

Now comes the fourth part. This is the part that changes for each site. Let's say we need a password for Google, so we'll make the forth part "Gggl." Our password for Google becomes "E@st3R_2015_Gggl." You might've noticed I removed the vowels from Google, but it's still memorable and readable. Or, you might choose to use an indirect reference to the site, such as "email," so the passphrase might become "E@st3R_2015_eMa!l."

If we had a Bank of America account, we might use "E@st3R_2015_Bof@m" or "E@st3R_2015_bank!ng" for a passphrase.

Of course, you can change the order of the different parts, maybe beginning with the site. The idea is to keep your pattern consistent across websites and accounts so you can have different passwords that are still memorable.

Using a pattern with certain set parts makes it easier to have long, complex passwords because all you really need to remember is the website/account part. While it's not a good idea to write your passwords down, if all you needed to write down was the fourth part—because the other three are the same for each site—then at least you wouldn't be writing the whole password for someone to steal. And, unless that someone knows your pattern, they would still be missing 12 or more characters.

This works well if you don't need to change your password frequently. So, what might we do to remember frequent password changes?

Secure systems should not remember any of your passwords in plain text. They should only store passwords in a hash format, which we'll discuss soon. That said, a change of a single character should change the hash enough so the system sees it as a different password.

As a caveat, I know of systems that limit how many numbers you can have. There are also systems that won't allow you to use your name, username, or other identifiable information.

In any case, you could add two or three digits or characters for the month the forced change happened. This becomes a fifth part of the passphrase. If the required change happens regularly, such as every 90 days, it shouldn't be too hard to remember when the last change was required.

Maybe the password change happened in January, so we'll use "Jan" for the fifth part. For simplicity, let's just insert this fifth part right before the site name, remembering to add the spacing character. Now the passphrase becomes "E@st3R_2015_Jan_bank!ng," which is a nice 23-character passphrase.

Another option for creating memorable passwords is to select four or five unrelated words. A common example found on the web is "correcthorsebatterystaple" or correct, horse, battery, staple if the words were separated. (Of course, don't use this example for your password.)

This approach is far better than using a single word, with some numbers and special characters. Its strength is its length, but it's missing some complexity. However, most people are only likely to select from about 3,000 common words.[2]

Hackers are getting smart to this method and can use password crackers to string several words together. Having 3,000 words to test, strung together in combinations of four and using lowercase letters, would only have about 101 trillion possibilities. Compare that to the eight-character password made of numbers, lowercase and uppercase letters, and special characters with around 218 trillion options. That may sound like a lot, but, in a few sections, you can see how quickly passwords can get cracked.

If you use several words together, make sure you add some uppercase letters, numbers, and special characters to the mix of lowercase letters. Maybe add a special character as the space and capitalize the last letter of each word. Or, alternate the words between lowercase and uppercase. The previous example might become "correct#HORSE#battery#STAPLE," which I think is easier to type than only capitalizing the ending letters.

Now that we've gone through some examples to create strong passphrases, wouldn't it be better to only have to remember a few passphrases and let something else manage the scores of others?

Easy-to-manage passwords

There is a way to easily manage your passwords while keeping them all unique, long, strong, and secure. The secret: use a password manager.

There are a lot of password managers available. You can purchase a password manager, subscribe to one, or find free ones.

Password managers can be installed on your device, launched as an independent application (where the application is not installed with the program files of the system), or in the cloud.

Because there are many possible password managers you could use (and you should probably limit yourself to one or maybe two if you want one for personal accounts and another for work-related ones), we won't be discussing the various possibilities. Before you decide on one, look for reviews and get some feedback. Some password managers are better than others. Just know that for creating and managing lots of secure passwords, you should really be using a password manager.

Password manager

There are several advantages to using a password manager.

First, you can create unique, strong, and secure passwords for every single website and account you have. The best part: you don't have to remember any of them.

The only passwords you really need to remember are the ones to log in to your computer and other devices and the one to log in to your password manager.

In the password manager I use, and many are similar, I simply click the login link by the account I want to open. The link opens the login page, and from there I just drag and drop the username and password into their respective fields. I click the login button on the site, and I'm in.

There are a few sites that don't allow me to drag and drop, but they do allow me to paste into the login fields. It's a little more work, but I'll just copy the username and password from the manager, paste them where they go, and log in. A couple sites don't allow the paste function. With these anomalies, I open the account information in the password manager to get the password.

Another advantage of the password manager is if there are security questions, I can store the answers to these questions in the notes of each account entry. Double-clicking the account in the password manager opens the entry and I can see the notes, just in case I can't remember the answer.

In the password manager, websites and accounts can be sorted into several default categories—like general, email, homebanking, education, and utilities—or I can create new categories.

If I don't feel like coming up with a unique, random password, the password manager has a password generator I can use to create truly unique, and very unmemorable, passwords. When generating a password, I can select what sets of characters I want (which I'll choose based on what the site allows), how many from each set, and a total length for the password.

Of course, I can always enter my own password, but it probably won't be as secure as the one the generator can create.

If a site requires a password change, I open the password manager, create a new password, copy it to the site for the new password, and save the changes.

If needed, the password manager has a history, so I can view old passwords. This has come in handy when, in the rare instance, I thought I'd changed a password, but the site was not recognizing the new password and I had to find the old password.

I started using a password generator in 2011, after I was introduced to one in late 2010. I was sold on the idea when I learned about it in class, but it took a few months before I actually tried it. I started using it more as an experiment, but I haven't looked back. It's been easy to use and easy to transfer to another computer; it easily helps me manage all the passwords I have created over the years.

How fast can a password be cracked?

The real answer is, it depends. If your password is one of those on the list the hacker is checking against, then the answer is too fast. Of course, it may take seconds or a few days to actually discover what your password is.

For fun, let's run some numbers.

Back in 2017, Intel introduced the Core i9 Extreme Edition processor that could perform 1 trillion computational operations every second. While this was billed as a consumer desktop chip, it cost $1,999,[4] which doesn't include the cost of the rest of the computer. Even a few years later, most consumer computer processors aren't quite that fast. But, for our example, let's use this processor, as it has a nice round number for our calculations.

To begin, we'll just leave the password as strictly numbers.

At 1 trillion calculations per second, a password consisting of four numbers (with only 10,000 possible combinations) would be broken faster than you could start and stop a stopwatch. If the password were 8 digits long, there are only 100 million combinations, which would, theoretically, take the processor less than a second to go through.

Bumping the password to 16 numbers long would increase the time to get through all the number combinations to a little less than 2.8 hours. We're starting to see the power of exponential strength.

A 20-digit password gives 100,000,000,000,000,000,000 possible combinations. Divide that by 1 trillion calculations per second, and it would take about 1,157 days to go through every combination. So, you have, at most, just over 3 years before the password gets cracked, assuming your password is the last on the list.

However, it's unlikely the cracker would have to go through every possible combination before getting to the correct password.

Let's add complexity to the password by including lowercase and uppercase letters and special characters, or a complexity base of 70.

A four-character password gives only 24,010,000 possible combinations; so, theoretically, the processor would get through all the possibilities in less than a second.

Doubling the password to eight characters gives over 576 trillion combinations. The time to crack the password would be 576.48 seconds, or just under 10 minutes. Are you feeling secure with your eight-character password?

Now let's increase the password to 16 characters long. The number of possible combinations is 3.32×10^{29} and it would take the processor over 332 quadrillion seconds—that's over 10.5 billion years to get through all the possibilities.

You should be feeling a little more secure with longer passwords. This is why I recommend a passphrase that's at least 16-characters long.

But, passphrase length isn't all that matters to security. No matter the passphrase's strength, it's not secure if you give it to someone (we'll take more about that when we discuss phishing).

Are passwords stolen in a data breach?

It seems to happen regularly. You hear the news, another data breach. It's almost a regular news staple, the latest in a long list of companies who have had user account information stolen.

The latest report isn't much different. Usernames, emails, and passwords were among the stolen information.

Then you realize you have an account with that organization.

This is probably the biggest reason to never use the same password for all your accounts. Since it's common for people to use the same username (especially because for many sites it's just an email address), if hackers get your password, they will try it with every possible site where you might have an account.

Using the same password for everything is equivalent to having one key for everything: your house, your work, your cars, your gun safe, your bank deposit box, etc. While it's convenient for you, it's extremely convenient for the criminal, especially if there's a list to all the locks that work with the key. If the hacker gets into your email, it's likely he'll find emails from various sites where you have accounts, which is almost like a list of places to try the username and password.

There is a possible silver lining in a data breach where passwords are stolen. In most cases, the plaintext, readable password was not what was stolen. What was stolen was the password hash.

What is a hash?

In cuisine, a hash is a chopped mixture of various foods, with the result looking nothing like any of the ingredients on their own. And, no matter how hard you try, you cannot reverse the process and return any of the ingredients to their original state.

The idea is similar with hashing a password. The plaintext password, which we can easily read, is entered into a hashing algorithm, or function. The algorithm applies various calculations and rules to the password to convert it into another value. This end value is called a hash.

The good news is, like a food hash, you cannot reverse the process. That is, if you have the password hash, you cannot simply run it backwards through the hashing function to get the original password. The hashing algorithm is a one-way street.

Here's the bad news. There are a lot of types of hashing functions, and many are not very secure. Unfortunately, some organizations still use old, insecure hashing algorithms.

So, why is it bad if the hash is a one-way process?

Let's go back to the food. The less secure hashes are like the simple chopped ham and potato hash. While you don't know exactly how much ham or potatoes the process started with, you can quickly perform a few hash attempts to see what matches. When your starting ingredients result in the same end hash, you know you have a match.

However, a real good hash might involve several types of meat, each chopped, diced, and minced different ways. For added flavor, some of the meats may be marinated or otherwise prepared. Then there are several vegetables, also chopped, diced, and minced. The end hash is very different from the basic ingredients and much more difficult to replicate.

Similarly, there are different kinds of hash functions. Some aren't very good, and others are much more secure. The type of algorithm your password runs through determines its strength.

Typically, an organization will use the same hashing function for all its passwords, mostly because it simplifies the programming. Changing to another algorithm incurs a lot of time and expense.

Some of the common cryptographic hash functions used are MD5, SHA-1, SHA-2, and SHA-3. Of those, MD5 is the least secure, and password hashes stored as MD5 hashes are the most vulnerable in a data breach. The Secure Hash Algorithm (SHA) hashes are much more secure, with version 3 being released by NIST in 2015. There are other hash functions, but these are more widely used.

You should know, there are lists of millions of passwords (the ingredients) freely available on the internet.

When password hashes are stolen, one of the first things to determine is what hashing function was used. If the hashing function is identified, a pre-existing list of passwords (and even just words found in a dictionary) can be run through the algorithm to see what matches are found.

A program that tries to find a hash's password is known as a password cracker. There are a lot of free password crackers, and even some websites where you can enter the hash and get the original characters that created the hash.

Many password crackers have special functions, such as trying password combinations while only using numbers for the first or last few characters. Therefore, it's recommended not to have numbers at the end of the password.

You don't need to know, or even be aware of, all the different cracking options. You just need to remember that password cracking becomes exponentially more difficult with longer and complex passwords, as discussed earlier.

If a hacker gets a stolen "password" list, most likely it's a list of password hashes. While you can't do anything about the hashing algorithm that was used, your objective is to make sure your password is as difficult to crack as possible.

Spicing up the password with "salt"

Even the most secure cryptographic hashing functions have a problem. If you and somebody else happen to use the same password, the hash for your password and the hash for their password will be the same.

In the eyes of the hacker, it's a two-for-one. And if more people have that same password, it's all the easier.

Returning to food, what do chefs do to make their recipe unique?

Up to this point, we've only mentioned the main ingredients. But, most recipes call for some spice. Truly unique dishes may add a secret sauce or mix of spices.

To make your password its own unique dish and further protect it, the most secure cryptographic systems will add what is known as a "salt" to the password. Every password is given a unique salt. The password plus salt then go through the hashing function together. In the end, if you have the same password as someone else, the resulting hash will still be different.

The hacker doesn't know the passwords are the same because the hashes are different. The only way to crack the passwords is to discover what each one is salted with.

So, if a data breach report mentions salted passwords, then you know there is an added level of security and protection for the passwords. That said, it's still a good idea to change your password for that account.

Hacked or compromised account?

We've discussed some measures you can take to become more secure. However, even after taking these measures, some hackers can still break in. How can you tell if your account has been hacked? These are two signs someone else has accessed your account:

- You notice unfamiliar activity on your account.
- Someone informs you of a suspicious email sent from your account.

Here are some of the steps you can take to secure a compromised account:

- Log in to your account.
- Review your account activity/history.
- Check and review what devices have connected and used the account, if the account provides this information.
- If you haven't done so already, enable two-factor authentication for the account.
- If the account has financial information—like a bank or credit card account—make sure there hasn't been any unauthorized and unfamiliar transactions, or instructions given to the institution, such as a money transfer or opening a new account.
- Make sure your anti-malware is up-to-date, and have it run a full scan on your device. Hopefully the anti-malware will be able to remove the malicious software. If not, you may have to reset the device.
- Make sure your browser is up-to-date.
- Change your password to a secure passphrase.

Checking for a compromised account

Because products change, I have tried to avoid mentioning specific products. However, when it comes to checking your username and password for possible compromises, there aren't a lot of options, particularly free ones.

Google has an extension for its Chrome browser, called Password Checkup. It takes the username and password entered, encrypts and hashes them multiple times (more on encryption and hashes later), and compares them against a list of four billion unsafe name and password combinations. Google calls the process "blinding" because it does not reveal any of your account details. If the process detects compromised username and password information, you're notified.

You can also manually check your accounts using your email address at the website https://haveibeenpwned.com/.

The "Have I Been Pwned" site is operated by Troy Hunt, a Microsoft regional director and security professional, who created the site as a free resource. "Pwned" (pronounced "poned") means "to get owned." The site's service checks your email to see if it is was in a breach. The following are two of my emails; the first was pwned, the next was not.

Figure 1: Email address has been pwned.

Figure 2: Email address was not found to be pwned.

A separate page on the site can check for "pwned" passwords.

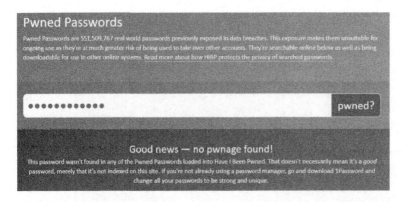

Figure 3: Password was not pwned.

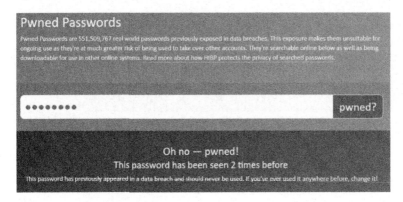

Figure 4: Password was pwned.

If you register your email with the site, you'll receive a notification if the email is discovered in a breach.

Welcome to Have I Been Pwned

You (or possibly someone else), just subscribed ███████████ to the notification service that will automatically let you know if your address is caught up in a future data breach. It's a free service and you can unsubscribe at any time if you don't want the notifications.

Just to confirm that you're a real person behind a real email address, click on the link below then you'll be automatically subscribed to new breach notifications where this email address has been pwned.

Verify my email

If you don't want to receive any future breach notifications, just click here to unsubscribe.

Figure 5: Email notification of subscribing to service.

The following is a recent email I received regarding one of my email addresses.

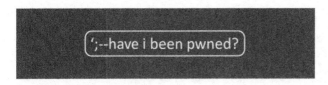

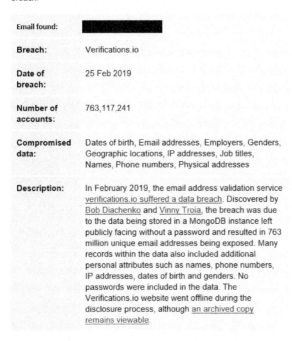

You've been pwned!

You signed up for notifications when your account was pwned in a data breach and unfortunately, it's happened. Here's what's known about the breach:

Email found:	████████████████
Breach:	Verifications.io
Date of breach:	25 Feb 2019
Number of accounts:	763,117,241
Compromised data:	Dates of birth, Email addresses, Employers, Genders, Geographic locations, IP addresses, Job titles, Names, Phone numbers, Physical addresses
Description:	In February 2019, the email address validation service verifications.io suffered a data breach. Discovered by Bob Diachenko and Vinny Troia, the breach was due to the data being stored in a MongoDB instance left publicly facing without a password and resulted in 763 million unique email addresses being exposed. Many records within the data also included additional personal attributes such as names, phone numbers, IP addresses, dates of birth and genders. No passwords were included in the data. The Verifications.io website went offline during the disclosure process, although an archived copy remains viewable.

Figure 6: Email notification of discovery of email being pwned.

I don't have any financial interest in the site—just the interest to help you keep safe.

Multi-factor authentication

Logging in to a system with only your username and password is known as a single-factor authentication. There are three general factors that can be used to authenticate someone. A system that uses more than one factor to authenticate users is generally more secure.

Authentication factor types

The first factor includes passwords and PINs (personal identification numbers). Secret answers to questions are also in this category. Even if the system you are logging in to requires a password, as well as answering a question or entering a PIN, the system only uses a single factor. Having to answer a question and/or enter a PIN makes the system a little more secure, but these requirements are all things you know. The problem is, the things you know are easily compromised, particularly if you write them down.

A second factor is something you have. This might be a smart card, or a USB dongle inserted into the computer. Your mobile phone can act as a second factor because it is something you have.

The weakness of this factor is the possibility of that something you have being stolen or lost.

However, combining something you know with something you have makes your account much more secure, and much less vulnerable to being hacked, because both factors are required to log in.

The third factor of authentication is what you are. This is a growing area of authentication. The most common forms of this factor are biometric attributes, such as fingerprints. Other forms of biometric attributes include retinal or iris scans, facial recognition, and voice recognition.

Other areas of "what you are" include behavioral or character traits. More complicated security systems might monitor how you walk (your gait). Or, the system might observe how you type something, like entering your password, to determine if it matches your usual typing.

More about different authentication methods (password, PIN, pattern swipes, facial recognition, and a few others) will be briefly discussed in Chapter 12, when we'll go into phone and mobile device security.

Regarding security questions

Security questions are often used when you log in to a site from a device that isn't recognized or when you need to reset a forgotten password.

Security questions really don't offer much additional security to your account, particularly if you use the real answers to the questions. Answers to a lot of these questions can be found by looking through someone's social media posts and information.

Some commonly used questions include:

- What is your mother's maiden name?
- What is the name of your first pet?
- What was your first car?
- What elementary school did you attend?
- What is the name of the town where you were born?
- What is your favorite food?

An in-depth analysis of security questions by researchers at Google found "that secret questions are neither secure nor reliable enough to be used as a standalone account recovery mechanism."[5] The reason is the answers to the questions "are either somewhat secure or easy to remember—but rarely both."[6]

Some of the findings of the research[7] include the following problems:

- Questions with common answers. For example, with a single guess, attackers had a 19.7 percent success rate in guessing answers to the "favorite food" question.
- Questions with few plausible answers, like asking a user who their favorite superhero is, where most people will select from a small set of answers.
- Questions where the answers are publicly available. The research found that 16 percent of the answers to security questions were

found on social networks. Other information can be found through public records, with one example being "at least 30% of Texas residents' mothers' maiden names can be deduced from birth and marriage records."[8]

The study found that partners, friends, or even acquaintances could correctly guess answers with five or less attempts.

Additionally, the Google study cited research that found 92 percent of users gave up answers to personal knowledge questions through email phishing.

So, what do we do? For accounts that require security questions, we still need to provide answers.

Some people give untruthful answers, believing it will be harder for someone to get the right answer. However, the Google study suggested that fake answers are more difficult to remember, leading to answers being written down which decreases security.

Unfortunately, there is not a perfect solution to answering security questions. The Google study did discover that answers longer than 10 characters tended to have greater memorability.

I have two recommendations where security questions are concerned.

First, if you use a password manager, and if the password manager has a place for notes about the account, keep your answers in the notes. This way you have your answers "written down," but they are more secure.

The second suggestion is to answer the question in a different way. Not exactly a fake answer, more of a misunderstanding answer.

For example, years ago a security question on one of my old accounts (before its security was upgraded) asked, "What color was your first car?"

It sounds like a good question, particularly for those who have had several cars and especially if those cars were owned before the internet and social media. But, think about how many people know what car you had. At least your friends and family.

Now consider how many colors there are. Yes, there are millions, but most people only really consider 16 to 32 different colors, so there likely isn't much to guess from where color is concerned.

So instead of answering that question about the *color* of my first car, my "misunderstanding" answer gave an answer to a similar question— "What was your first car?"

Common two-factor authentication

Two-factor authentication, which normally uses something you know (your password) and something you have (like a smartphone), is becoming more commonplace. Some organizations require it. Others allow users to opt in.

Some methods of using a mobile device as a second factor include a text or email to be sent with a limited-use code. This code is then entered on a separate login page. A couple of the financial institutions I know have incorporated this functionality.

The method might be a smartphone application, which is what my employer uses. After logging in to the organization's webpage with my username and password, a notice is sent to the application on my smartphone. My phone is tied to my account, and I simply approve the access request to get in. Should someone else try to log in with my username and password, the access request is sent to my phone, and I can deny the request.

Another possible method for two-factor authentication is the use of a key fob that provides a one-time use code that is entered on the second-factor page.

If your organization, or the account you use, offers the option for two-factor (or multi-factor) authentication, it's in your best interest to opt in. The initial setup usually doesn't take long. Normally it involves verifying a valid email, text, or setting up an application on a smartphone. The little bit of time to set up the second factor is well worth the added security.

Possible future authentication

As cybersecurity progresses, one of the critical elements is to ensure only authenticated users access the various systems they are authorized to access. Because of identity theft and stolen credentials, keeping the bad guys out is increasingly challenging. In the near future, we will see an increasing push for multi-factor authentication. Two-factor will become common, and most systems will require it. More sensitive systems will require multi-factor authentication.

Lip reading

While computers have been learning to understand the spoken word, and some systems have been learning to lip read, a new method of authentication is integrating the unique way individuals speak with passwords. Of the various lip reading authentication platforms, one is called LipPass, and it "deciphers the subtle yet distinct differences in how a user's mouth moves when they speak with 90.2 percent accuracy, and detects spoofers with 93.1 percent accuracy."[9]

While lip reading authentication isn't new, the reliability of this method is.

In one study published in January 2019, lip reading authentication was tested on four different smartphones, and "volunteers used the platform in four distinct environments, ranging from a well-lit, quiet laboratory to a dark, noisy pub."[10] The experiments compared LipPass to WeChat and Alipay.

In the controlled lab environment, LipPass had an accuracy of 95.3 percent, which was comparable to WeChat's voiceprint recognition accuracy of 96.1 percent and Alipay's face recognition accuracy of 97.2 percent. The difference showed in the other environments. Where LipPass's accuracy remained fairly constant, WeChat's accuracy dropped to 21.3 percent in noisy environments, and Alipay accuracy was 20.4 percent in dark environments.

Spoofers trying to hack these systems had a less than 10 percent success rate.

The bio-factor combination

Among these multi-factor systems, we will likely begin seeing combination systems. One likely possibility is a biometric implant, such as a small chip being inserted into a hand.

Currently there are some organizations, more common in Europe than in America, that allow employees to opt in and have small rice-sized chips inserted in the fleshy part of the hand, between the thumb and index finger. These chips replace access cards—the user just swipes his hand over the sensor to open the door—and can be used for mobile payment.[11]

Currently the chips are fairly limited in their ability, but as technology continues to advance, and costs come down, these chips will become more individualized. A driving factor will be the need to securely identify, authenticate, and authorize a user for a secure system.

The combination of an identification chip (something you have) with your body (something you are) provides two factors, and the chip isn't likely to get lost. It's likely that future chips will be personalized, and possibly biometrically assigned, and also include other functionality, like medical monitoring. Combined with a passphrase (or something else you know), an identification chip will incorporate a secure form of authentication.

While there are some who have religious issues with these chips, the fact is, they will become commonplace in the near future.[12]

CHAPTER 4

Backups

Backups are insurance for your data.

Homeowners, renters, flood, earthquake, and car insurance all have a common denominator: people get them not because they want to use them but just in case they need them.

You need to back up the data on your computer and other devices, not because you have to back it up—or even expect to use it—but just in case you need it. And, just like you regularly renew insurance and pay regular premiums, you need to make regular data backups.

Since most of us can't do much about the backups of an organization's data, our focus will be on the computing devices you use, such as your mobile phone and computer.

Several years ago, about a month after getting my first smartphone, I had the phone in my pocket when I heard it say something like "erasing data." I don't remember the exact words, but I remember quickly taking my phone out of my pocket and seeing the message that the data had been erased.

To put it mildly, I was upset. I had really cute videos of our children on it. I had not yet set up the automatic cloud backup (which was another expense), and I had not connected my phone to the computer to copy the videos.

All I can figure is that, by default, the operating system was set to delete data after 10 failed login attempts, and the phone must have had 10 failed login attempts in my pocket. Interestingly, while I have since been more diligent about backing things up, I never had that experience again, even though I had the phone for four more years, and I frequently put it in the same pocket.

Anyway, having backups of your data is always a good idea. And, it's one the three main things users can do to protect themselves from the effects of malware. The other two are having an updated and working anti-malware program and keeping the operating system and applications up-to-date.

Types of backup

There are many backup variations, but they all fall into three general categories: full, incremental, and differential.

The best type of backup is the full backup. But, full backups take longer to make and require more storage space. Most backup applications will do a full backup to start and another after a set time period. In between full backups, they will make incremental and/or differential backups.

Incremental backups are a backup of all changes made *since the last backup of any type*.

Differential backups back up files changed *since the last full backup*.

As mentioned, typical backup systems incorporate a variety of the three backups.

One example could be a full backup being created every Sunday. On Monday and Tuesday, incremental backups are made, which only back up the changes made each day. On Wednesday a differential back is made, which backs up all the changes made since Sunday, the last full backup. Thursday and Friday would be more incremental backups, saving changes made each of those days. Saturday might be another differential backup, and this time it would again back up all the changes made since Sunday, which was the last full backup. Another full backup happens the next day, Sunday.

It should also be noted that organizations will usually maintain several previous full backups before those backups are erased or sent off to a storage archive.

The frequency and types of backups are determined by how much storage space is required, how quickly the data needs to be recovered, and how quickly the organization can return to full-speed operations. For most organizations, cost is often the deciding factor.

Full backups are the quickest to restore, but they require the most storage space. The more frequent a full backup is made; the more space is required.

Incremental backups are the quickest to make and take up the least amount of space. But, they take the most time to restore because the previous full backup needs to be restored first, then all the subsequent incremental backups would be restored, in the right order, to fully restore the data.

If a differential backup is in place, the last full backup is restored first, then the latest differential backup, followed by any incremental backups made since the differential.

Because small organization don't usually have large amounts of data, they might have full daily backups without high storage space costs.

For individuals, full backups are usually best, although frequency depends on the individual's needs and circumstances.

For personal backups, the process is generally fairly simple. Most backup applications don't require you to know the difference between incremental, differential, or other types of backups. Usually you specify what you want backed up and how frequently, and the application backs it up. The backup application then checks for changes at the specified frequency and backs up the changes. Most flash drives, and even many portable hard drives, come with a backup utility/application you can install.

While these applications are usually easy to use, if you want to access the backed-up files, you need to go through the application. This usually means you have to launch the backup application to view or restore the files.

Personally, I like to select the folders and files I want to backup and paste them in the backup location. It's not elegant. It's not automatic. It doesn't even happen regularly. But, I can access them those files from another computer without having to run the application. This method works well for general data, like photos, music, and videos, but it's not the best option for sensitive data, which should be encrypted. We'll discuss encryption in Chapter 6.

Backup frequency

Your backup schedule really depends on your needs. If your data changes frequently, your backup schedule should reflect how much data you are willing to lose—or, more correctly, not lose.

When deciding on a backup frequency, ask yourself some of the following questions to gauge how much data you create and what your data loss tolerance may be. How many new files, or changes to files, do you make in day, or a week? How long did it take you to create the document, and do you have time to re-create it? Can you afford to redo a day's worth of work? How about a week's worth of work? Which would you be sadder about, losing a few photos or hundreds? How many photos do you take in a day or week?

The downtime needed to restore backups and recreate any missing data files should be a gauge in determining your backup schedule.

On a personal level, backups should happen regularly enough that you won't lose too much, if anything. The time and computing resources to perform the backup probably won't conflict too much with your use of the device, especially if you schedule backups for times when you aren't using the device.

On the business side, backup scheduling may be more complicated, especially if the operation runs around the clock. Storage space is a consideration, as is the use of computer resources needed to back up the data.

Downtime and loss of revenue may be factors. Where a small or medium business may not lose too much if their systems are down for a day, a large organization could lose millions for even a short downtime.

In each case, the costs and risks need to be evaluated and balanced. There are systems with an almost guarantee of near-immediate business continuity, but the cost of that type of backup system, with multiple redundant systems and off-site systems ready to go into action the moment the main systems go down (a hot site), may not be justified. The company may find that if they are able to restore business systems within an hour (or some other time period), they may lose less during that timeframe than they would spend maintaining a hot site.

Most individuals don't need the immediate or near-immediate restoration of data. But the length of time you can be without your data and the amount of data you could potentially lose since the last backup should be considered when deciding planning your backup schedule.

Where are your backups?

The location where you keep your backup makes a difference. It's important to note that your backup should not be on the same drive as the data that's being backed up.

We'll generalize backup locations as being either local or cloud based.

Local backups can be on portable storage devices, like flash drives or portable/external hard drives. Or, they can be local network storage locations. Most people don't have local network storage, but there are dedicated storage devices you can connect to your network. Some of these network devices will connect directly to a router. Other people may have a file server on their network. In any case, you know where these local backups are.

Cloud-based backup resources come in a variety of options, but they fit into two general categories. First are actual backup solutions. You install an application on your device, and the application sends backup data to the cloud storage.

The second category is just cloud-based storage, where you store copies of your files in the cloud. Services like Dropbox, Box, Apple's iCloud, Microsoft's OneDrive, and Google Drive are examples of the dozens of cloud-based storage options. Most of these options offer a limited free account. A common free limit is from 5 to 15 gigabytes of data storage. It sounds like a lot, until you realize how quickly photos, music, and videos gobble up storage space. After the free tier, there are varying storage levels you can subscribe to.

The advantage of cloud-based storage is you can get to it from anywhere you have internet access. The downside is you need internet service to access those files.

A big disadvantage to backing up files to a cloud service is that it can take a long time, especially with a slow internet connection.

Another benefit to cloud-based storage is that if a disaster strikes, you will almost certainly be able access those files from another location, provided there's internet service. Local backup storage may be susceptible to damage or may be destroyed by a local disaster.

However, having a local backup is advantageous in a few ways. First, you know where your backup is. With cloud storage you won't know where it is. Second, because you know where your local backup is, you also have control of your data. Entrusting your data to an online storage provider is trusting their system to be secure and to keep your data protected.

The biggest advantages of local backups are speed and cost.

At the time of this writing, a 4-terabyte (that's 4,000 gigabytes) portable hard drive costs less than $100. I found a 5 TB one for $99.99. A simple 256 GB flash drive costs less than $40.

Comparing that to the cloud, one current cloud storage option is $19.99 per year (or $23.88 if you go with the $1.99 monthly plan) for 100 GB of storage. Bumping it to 200 GB costs an extra $10. It's not a bad price for the convenience of cloud storage. It comes out to about 15 cents per GB per year for the 200 GB plan.

However, the 256 GB flash drive costs 15.6 cents per GB, and you pay for it only once. The 5 TB portable hard drive sets you back 1.9 cents per GB.

If you're on the road a lot or going to school or you just use your device a lot when you're not home, then backing up your files to a cloud-based storage may make better sense, mostly due to the convenience.

However, if you primarily use your computer at home, and your mobile device is backed up or synced to your computer frequently, then a local storage might be the better option.

How you choose to back up your data is up to you; just please, back up your files.

Check backups

Regardless of how you choose to back up your files, you should check your backups regularly.

In Chapter 2, I mentioned hardware lifespan. That lifespan becomes critically important when it comes to backing up your data. The older the hardware is, the more likely it is to fail, and you'll likely lose any data on that device.

If your computer/device is three years or older and you haven't backed up your data to a newer storage device, you should do so.

If your computer is over five years old, any data stored on it is on borrowed time. If you haven't backed up your data, you need to do it now.

Hopefully you have already been backing up your data. But if you haven't, consider this your call to action.

If you have, keep in mind that your backup drives are hardware and will eventually fail as well. If the drive is used frequently, it should be replaced every 3-5 years. A rarely used drive should last much longer.

That said, some of my flash drives, which were not used very much, have had issues when I tried using them after several years. Others work without a problem, though their 1 or 2 GB size is too small to be useful anymore.

This comes back to the need to check your backups. You shouldn't have to open every backed-up file. But, you should occasionally try to open one of them. It's a disheartening feeling when you think you have a backup, only to discover the flash drive won't respond or the files are corrupted and won't open.

Recovery

On one of the systems I manage, I create a backup of the entire system. If a failure occurs, I use the backup to quickly restore the system. There isn't much data change on the system, which means I don't make many backups of the system.

However, for personal use I only back up my data files. I generally recommend only backing up files, and not applications, or the full system.

The reason is, if there is a problem with any of the system files, such as from corrupted files or malware, I don't want to restore a backed-up copy of the system with those problems. It may take longer, but I'd rather start over with a clean system, installing whatever applications are needed, and then restore the data.

My recommendation for backups

My recommendation is to have at least two backup sources.

The first backup, which will be the more frequent backup, can be to a portable hard drive, network drive, or cloud-based storage that is regularly connected to the system. The frequency of your backup should be based on how often your data changes (including new and modified files) and how much data you can tolerate losing.

The second backup also needs to occur on a regular basis, but the data should be backed up to a storage device that is not normally connected to your computer.

This second form of backup is beneficial because some advanced forms of malware attack more than just the C: drive and other common drives. These varieties of malware look for any storage attached to the computer, whether it is physically or virtually connected. Some variants of ransomware (more on these in Chapter 7) look for files and encrypt them so you can't access them until you pay a ransom and get a code to unlock them.

With many forms of malware, the best recourse is to wipe the device and start over from scratch, reinstalling the operating system and all the applications. This process also wipes all the data from the device.

If all your data is on the infected device, it will be gone. If your attached backup was also infected by the malware, it will also need to be wiped. But, the odds of safely recovering data are better if the backup was not connected to the device at the time of the malware infection.

Some will say the more backups, the better. But, there is a cost with having more backups.

Taking into consideration the anticipated hardware lifespan, you might consider replacing one backup drive at least every other year. That way one of the backup drives is less than two years old. If one of the drives fail (most likely the older one), you should still have service life in the other drive, and some time to get a replacement.

CHAPTER 5

Updates and Upgrades

Among the best practices in cybersecurity is the need to keep the operating system and applications on your system up-to-date. This does not mean running an outdated (and unsupported) operating system, or old application, with all the updates that are available for that old system.

This also isn't an endorsement to necessarily go out and buy the latest version.

However, if the developer is no longer actively supporting and providing patches for the operating system or application, then it is time to upgrade to a newer version.

Operating system

The operating system, or OS, is what manages all the programs, drivers, and applications.

When you power on the computer, the system runs a check on the hardware to see what's connected and working. On most machines, the computer then launches the operating system.

Microsoft Windows is the most common OS, with the different versions of Windows accounting for more than 80 percent of the computers used. It's estimated there are 1 billion Windows-based machines around the world, with 400 million using Windows 10.

Apple's computer operating system, known as Mac OS (or OS X), is the second most popular system with nearly 100 million active Mac users.

Less than two percent of the computers run a version of a Linux-based operating system, and most of these machines are servers and not personal computers.

In the mobile device market, the Android OS has the greater market share of between 80 and 90 percent. Apple's iOS is on most of the remaining mobile device systems. A small percentage of mobile devices use other operating systems.

The OS, regardless of which one, manages the various processes and applications.

You could consider the OS as the landlord of an apartment complex, and the applications are tenants. Part of OS's job is to manage how the tenants work and interact with the complex. The OS makes sure the tenants neither overuse various resources nor access off-limit resources. If there's a problem, the OS tries to correct it and may have to close the application.

Keeping the OS up-to-date is one of the primary ways to protecting your system from security threats.

Ideally, your OS should not allow you to install non-approved applications. At the very least, it should prompt you before, and make sure you approve of, an application installation. This is like having a pre-qualified tenant wanting to get a space in the complex. Installing only OS-manufacturer-approved applications is like having a clean background check on a potential tenant. While not a guarantee of perfect tenancy, it helps ensure the safety of the system.

Update vs. upgrade

Sometimes "update" and "upgrade" get confused. While updates and upgrades may have some overlap, this is a general difference.

An *update* makes changes to the current version.

Updates are usually free. They are often fixes, or patches, for problems. Sometimes they include the addition of new or improved features. Sometimes a version of the software will have a major update, which is almost like an upgrade.

An *upgrade* replaces the product with a newer version.

Usually there's a cost to upgrade to the next, or newer, version.

Before you upgrade, or perform any major update, it's important to remember to back up your data. Some systems will create a restore point, but it's still a good idea to make your own backup and not rely on the restore point.

When it comes to upgrading to a new operating system, I prefer to install the new OS on a clean machine. Not physically clean, with the dust wiped off, although that is nice. But "clean" meaning the drive has been erased or wiped clean of all the data.

First, I'll back up the data and make note of all the installed applications that I use. If there's an application installed but not used, I don't want to clutter the new system with it. Before the OS installation, I'll make sure the hard drive is wiped/erased. My experience is a new OS version runs better on a clean drive. Installing an OS on a clean drive is sometimes referred to as a fresh install.

A fresh install may be less convenient than upgrading an existing OS. If you don't do a fresh install, your data (should) still be there after the upgrade. You don't have to re-install the applications, and application-specific configurations should still exist.

However, OS upgrades can also cause applications to stop working. There may be a compatibility issue between the new OS and an older application, which you should check for these issues before deciding to upgrade. With compatibility issues, the old application can sometimes be installed on a newer OS by running the installer and application in a compatibility mode.

Similar to applications, some drivers for peripherals may have issues with a new OS. Some older printers in my workplace require the driver to be installed using the compatibility mode on a newer OS.

Another problem with upgrading a current OS to a new version without a fresh install is the system can become further cluttered, which doesn't help performance issues.

My experience is major OS upgrade versions run better and faster with a fresh install, on a wiped hard drive. A fresh install has even brought older computers back to a satisfactory working condition.

The other advantage of a fresh install, which is related to security, is any problems or potential problems that may have been on the old system shouldn't be an issue with a clean OS install.

Antivirus/anti-malware

Technically these applications are anti-malware, as they target all kinds of malware, but most people refer to them as an antivirus. Antivirus and anti-malware will be used interchangeably.

Before we go on, a word of caution. No anti-malware product will catch 100 percent of all malware. If the vendor makes that claim, don't trust them. However, some anti-malware solutions do stop a very high percentage of malware. Even some free versions do a fantastic job.

A good anti-malware product will do two things. First, the anti-malware is like another background check on a tenant. It checks the validity of the program and compares the program to a list of known malware signatures.

Second, the antivirus should monitor how various processes and applications are acting. Malicious behavior should be identified and quarantined.

Because there are hundreds of thousands of new malicious files detected every day, it's vital that your antivirus is kept up-to-date.

More will be discussed about antivirus/anti-malware solutions in the Chapter 7.

Keep applications up-to-date

Malware often targets security holes in popular applications, through which they can infect a computer or mobile device. Although there are many possible problems, these security holes might be a section of poorly written code or an issue in the way the application interacts with the OS or a piece of hardware.

The more popular the application, the more of a target it becomes for cybercriminals. Outside of foreign cyberspies targeting specific government agencies or industries, most malware threats target as many potential victims as they can. This means going after the popular operating systems and applications.

Popular applications include web browsers, like Chrome, Safari, and Internet Explorer. They also include common free applications, such as Adobe Reader, Adobe Flash, and Oracle's Java—especially older versions of these applications.

Commonly purchased applications, like Microsoft Office, are also targets for hackers.

Many of these application threats come from opening a file that is associated with the application, such as using Adobe Reader or Adobe Acrobat to open an infected PDF document.

Just like your antivirus, the various applications (including web browsers) need to be kept up-to-date.

Keeping your operating system, antivirus, and applications updated can help protect your devices from malicious programs, especially from the millions of malware that exploit vulnerabilities in outdated software.

CHAPTER 6

Encryption

Encryption is simply converting easily understood information into something that isn't easy to understand.

A simple letter-number substitution is an elementary form of encryption, but it's easily broken when you discover the code, such as "1" being substituted for "A," "2" for "B," and so on. Or, maybe the letters are offset, with the "A" being represented by "C," "B" by "D", and so on with the letters Y and Z being represented by A and B, respectively.

Varying forms of encryption, often referred to as coded (or encoded) information, have existed for millennia. Military generals have employed it to communicate secret plans to their front-line commanders. Spies have used encryption to smuggle out state secrets.

Expanding on this, we can say that encryption is the process of encoding information in a way that only an authorized recipient is able to decode.

In Chapter 3, we reviewed hashing. Hashing protects the password by making them unreadable.

Encryption serves a similar function—to make data unreadable. However, unlike password hashes—where the hash cannot be reversed to reveal the password—encryption requires the ability to reverse the process, to decrypt the data.

"Encryption is the process of applying a mathematical function to a file that renders its contents unreadable and inaccessible—unless you have the decryption key."[13] The basic process of encryption begins with an encryption algorithm and a key. The key, often a password, is the secret ingredient to the encrypting process. Once there is a key, the data can be encoded into its encrypted format.

The encrypted data is protected from unauthorized viewers, who would only see an indecipherable mess of characters if they were to access it.

An authorized user can then use a key (sometimes the same key, sometimes different one, depending of the type of encryption) to unlock and decrypt (decode) the data back into a readable, plaintext format.

In computer cryptography, encryption has evolved into a complex science. While we will not go into depth of any type of encryption, it is important to know some of the basic types.

Some encryption terms

Before we go more into encryption, we need to define some terminology.

Let's start with plaintext, which is the plain, human-readable message. It's unsecured data on a system that anyone can read, if they can find it. A similar term is cleartext. Both are unencrypted information. While they are synonymous, plaintext is usually applied to information before it goes through cryptographic algorithms; cleartext is the information that is stored or transmitted unencrypted, or data that is "in the clear."

The encryption algorithm is sometimes referred to as a cipher. Thus, after being encrypted, the data is called ciphertext. Ciphertext looks like random, meaningless characters.

Just as we use a key to unlock a locked door, a cryptographic key is needed to unlock, or decrypt, an encrypted file. Often this key is a password.

In the physical world there are various types of locks, and we could consider each lock type as a different encryption algorithm. It's hard to suppress the details of how an encryption function works, just as how a lock works usually isn't a secret. But, security of the lock is in keeping the key safe.

For the decryption process to work, the corresponding decrypting algorithm is needed along with the correct key.

While a password is a key, a key is not always a password. The difference is a key is created by an algorithm, and a password is normally created by a user. Sometimes passwords are used to help create a cryptographic key. In any case, the key is needed in the decryption process to revert the ciphertext back into plaintext.

Hashes were discussed in the Chapter 3. Creating a hash is similar to the encryption process, where an algorithm is used to make the calculation. But unlike encryption, which can be decrypted, there's isn't a "de-hashing" key, as the hashing process cannot be reversed.

When using encryption, hashing can be useful in verifying the integrity of a file. If a file is run through a hashing algorithm, a hash value is calculated for the file. The file itself isn't hashed; there's just a hash value for the file. If any piece of the file is changed, whether intentionally or accidentally (such as through data corruption), when the file hash is computed again the resulting value will be different. Knowing the hash of a file is useful if you download a file and want to make sure it's a valid copy of the original, or if it's been corrupted or tampered with.

In Chapter 3 we also talked about salt. As a brief review, salting involves adding a unique value to the one-way hash function. The addition of the salt makes the hash value of your password completely unique from any other user who might use the same password.

There are two general types of encryption, and many different implementations of each. The two main types are symmetric and asymmetric.

In symmetric encryption, the same key is used for both the encryption and decryption functions. If you encrypt the files on your computer, the same password is used to lock and unlock the files.

While symmetric encryption works great for securing personal files or communicating securely with one (or very few) person(s), it is not practical for secure communication with a lot of people. If symmetric encryption were used, it would be like sharing your password with everyone you would want to communicate with, and it becomes easy for your password to be stolen.

The other type of encryption is asymmetric, and it uses two different keys. One key is called a public key, and the other is a private key. This form of encryption is also called public key cryptography, and it is the basis of the majority of secure (encrypted) communication used with online services.

Asymmetric encryption is much more practical for use in securing communication. When a public and private key are created, the public key can be sent for anyone to use, but the private key is kept secret and protected. Together, the public and private key are known as a key pair.

The public key is used to encrypt the message. But, the paired private key is needed to decrypt the message. So, anyone can create an encrypted message, but only the person (or site) with the private key can decrypt it.

When you access a website that has "HTTPS" at the beginning, the site is using a secure (which is what the "S" is for) encryption protocol. The communication between your computer and the site is encrypted, typically using a protocol called Transport Layer Security (TLS).

The HTTPS encryption process begins with asymmetric encryption, using both private and public keys. When you access the site, these keys are then used to create a single-use symmetric key for your secure connection to that site.

A majority of websites now use HTTPS connections instead of HTTP. Knowing the difference between HTTPS and HTTP connections can help you identify whether a site you visit is encrypting the communication between your device and the site.

There are several symmetric and asymmetric algorithms in use, with some being less secure than others. Most users don't need to know the various types. However, it's helpful to be aware of the more common ones, if for no other reason than to know it's an encryption algorithm.

The Advanced Encryption Standard (AES) is a symmetric algorithm and is currently the encryption choice of the government for protecting classified information. It has good functionality across a wide range of hardware, meaning the encryption/decryption process doesn't use as much processing power as some other algorithms.

The most common asymmetric algorithm used on secure websites is Rivest-Shamir-Adleman (RSA). RSA is slow, but it's only used when establishing a secure web connection. RSA is used to create symmetric keys, which are then used to encrypt and decrypt the web communications between the site and your device.

For computing hash values (digests) for files, the more common algorithms are MD5, SHA-1, SHA-2, and SHA-3. MD5 is an older hash function and isn't as secure as the Secure Hashing Algorithms (SHA), with SHA-3, released in 2015, being the more secure of these three functions. However, while MD5 may not be a good choice for securing a password, it's valuable for calculating the hash digest for a file.

For personal use, symmetric encryption is typically used.

Where can encryption be used?

Encryption can be used just about anywhere, including files, folders, and entire disks. Just remember, accessing those files requires decryption first, which usually involves entering a password.

When decrypting files, there may be a little lag time before an encrypted file is decrypted or for a file to become encrypted. The lag time is just the computer running the file through the process. This computational lag is more noticeable on older, slower computers. For most users, the encryption/decryption process is hardly noticeable.

Many flash drives and portable hard drives have an encryption application on them. On some drives you can run the application from the drive, without installing anything on the computer.

Because there a lot of applications you can use for encrypting your data, we're not going to discuss them. However, you should be aware that both Apple and Microsoft have built-in encryption features in their operating systems. In the Mac OS, the encryption feature is called FileVault. On Windows 10 the encryption feature is BitLocker.

For whatever encryption system you choose to use, please refer to user information and guides, as specific details and instructions are outside the scope of this book. That said, don't be afraid of using them; they are fairly user friendly.

Why is encryption needed?

By now, the value of encryption should be apparent. If you have information you want kept safe, your best option is to make it unreadable.

While photos, music, and video files probably don't need to be encrypted, you likely have sensitive information on your computers and other devices. This information may be tax returns, financial statements (banking, credit cards, investments), Social Security numbers, and other information that could be of value. Encrypting your sensitive information can keep curious eyes from seeing and maliciously using it. And, if your device becomes infected with malware, encryption can provide additional protection against unauthorized use.

Remember the integrity part of the CIA security triad? Encryption play a major role in protecting the confidentiality and integrity of your data.

CHAPTER 7

Malware

Malware, short for malicious software, is a broadly applied term for a variety of malicious programs. A "virus" is a particular form of malware, although most people just use "virus" to refer to any computer infection.

Cybercriminals use malware for many reasons, including to:

- Steal sensitive personal, business, proprietary, or financial information.
- Disrupt normal system operations.
- Spy.
- Lock files on the victim's system and hold them for ransom.
- Perform attacks on other systems, including distributed-denial-of-service (DDoS) attacks.
- Gain unauthorized access to a system.
- Send spam and other emails.

Malware is normally installed and runs on your computer, smartphone, or other device without your knowledge and/or consent. It can get onto your system by a variety of methods, including email, web pages and links, and infected USB drives.

Most malware is designed to take advantage of (exploit) a vulnerability, usually found on an application or the operating system. Most vulnerabilities that are discovered should get a patch from the developer, particularly if the application is a popular one.

Many larger developers have teams looking for vulnerabilities. Some larger companies have a bug bounty program, where they pay people for finding and reporting the problem to their team.

When a vulnerability is discovered and exploited before the developer is aware of it, it's known as a zero-day exploit because the developer has had zero days to patch it. The longer a zero-day is kept hidden, the longer the cybercriminals exploit it.

In 2015, Symantec reported there was about one zero-day exploit discovered each week.[14] However, with ever-increasing numbers of applications and complexity of software, zero-day vulnerabilities will become more common. Cybersecurity Ventures "predicts that system break-ins made through a previously unknown weakness . . . will average one per day in the United States by 2021."[15]

General types

While malware can perform more than one purpose, most malware is categorized by its main function or how it attacks the system.

Adware

More than just unwanted (and often annoying) advertisements, adware is usually installed with free downloads, and then the adware may install additional software on the system. The adware itself may, or may not, be of a malicious nature, but that's not always the case for the applications and plug-ins it may download and install.

Botnet

A bot is the malware, and the botnet is a group of computers infected with the same malware. Once installed, the bot will communicate with a command-and-control server, waiting for further instructions. A botnet is often used in a DDoS attack, or to send out spam.

The Necurs botnet, which is operated by a worldwide cybercrime gang, was the primary distributor of malware in 2018, including ransomware and banking trojans.[16]

Botnets are a big problem, and they were involved in nearly 40,000 successful data breaches on financial and insurance companies.[17]

DDoS attack

The DDoS, or distributed-denial-of-service, attack is not actually malware, but it can be the result of certain malware, related to botnets, being installed on a device.

You could compare a DDoS to a large protest outside of a retail store. You want to go in to shop, but the large amount of people outside the doors makes it difficult to enter. Other legitimate shoppers may also try to get in, and maybe a few manage to gain access to the doors. Because of the inaccessibility, you may decide to just try back later.

A DDoS occurs when an excessive amount of web inquiries is made on a web server, usually targeting a website. The unexpected, and overwhelming, amount of web requests on the site can cause the site to slow, fail to respond, or crash the server. The result is that legitimate traffic to the site is restricted or even denied. If the DDoS extends over time, it can cost a busy ecommerce site a lot of money.

In a DDoS, the command and control server sends out instructions to all the devices on the botnet to attack a website. The devices then start sending access requests to the victim. When the site responds with an acknowledgement to continue the web communication, the botnet device ignores the acknowledgement, and sends another connect request, which leaves the original request open for a short time. The site can quickly get too many open requests, and it's still trying to field more requests than it can handle.

The good news is many DDoS attacks don't often last as long as they used to. Many websites, especially the popular ones, can quickly scale up to handle increasing requests. Detection of these attacks has also improved, allowing organizations to better defend against them.

Information stealer

This category of malware includes various malware designed to steal sensitive data or keystrokes. Examples include key loggers, spyware, sniffers, and form grabbers.

Ransomware

Ransomware is "malware that holds the system for ransom by locking users out of their computer or by encrypting their files."[18]

Ransomware was first mentioned in the 2013 Verizon Data Breach Investigations Report; in the report, ransomware was involved in less than 5 percent of the malware incidents. In the 2017 report, ransomware was the "most prevalent variety of malicious code,"[19] being used in more than 40 percent of malware incidents.

A 2018 Ponemon Institute report revealed that 67 percent of 1,100 senior information technology professionals believe "the risk of cyber extortion and data breaches will increase in frequency."[20]

Rootkit

Rootkits gives the attacker administrator privileges (also called root privileges) to the system. They may also actively attempt to hide from other software, like an antivirus, and even the operating system.

Trojan

Named after the mythological Trojan horse, trojans disguise themselves as a normal program and trick users into installing them on the system. Once inside the system, the trojan will "perform malicious actions such as stealing sensitive data, uploading files to the attacker's server, or monitoring webcams."[21] Like other categories of malware, there are various classes of trojans, such as a remote access trojan or a downloader/dropper trojan.

Backdoor or remote access trojan

A remote access trojan (RAT) is a class of trojan that gives the attacker access to the compromised system.

Downloader or dropper

This class of trojan downloads and installs other software, usually malware, onto the system.

Virus

A virus is malware that can copy itself but that requires user interaction to spread it to other systems.

Worm

Like viruses, worms can replicate themselves; but, unlike viruses, they can spread on their own, infecting other systems without user interaction.

Cryptojacking

The last several years have seen ransomware become popular in cyberattacks. "However, more recently, criminals seem to use less ransomware and are instead increasingly leveraging coin-mining malware."[22]

What is "coin-mining"? It's known as cryptojacking, and the cybercriminal infects your device with malware designed to "mine" cryptocurrency.

In cryptocurrency, complex math problems are calculated to check ledger history and approve transactions. Cryptominers use vast arrays of computing equipment to perform these calculations. The miner must first verify a transaction. Then, to add a new block of transactions, a seriously complex computational math problem, called a "proof of work," needs to be solved. Producing the correct answer, which is actually a hash value, is a gamble. Currently the odds of a miner getting the right hash value is less than 1 in 6 trillion.[23] But the trick is not just getting the right value but being the first to do so. These calculations require a lot of computing power, and successful miners can earn cryptocurrency in exchange for the use of their mining systems—if they're the first to get the right value.

Legitimate miners have their own systems to perform the mining calculations. Those operating illicitly try to install cryptojacking malware on as many devices as possible. Installing this malware on other devices spreads the workload, increases their access to computational power, increases their chances to be the first in coin-mining. Of course, if you have cryptojacking malware on your device you don't get any credit for it.

There are other problems with cryptojacking. If you have cryptojacking malware on your device, it uses your device's resources. The CPU becomes over-taxed, which slows down your device and could even make it overheat. The increased use also requires more electricity and can decrease your battery time. If your device, or system, is infected with cryptojacking malware, it may indicate your network has been breached, and you could be vulnerable to other threats.

Why isn't software secure to begin with?

The 2017 Application Security Report, published by Cybersecurity Ventures, estimated "there are 111 billion lines of new software code generated by developers every year."[24] That works out to over 2 billion lines of code each week.

The estimate at the beginning of 2018 was there were about 22.3 million software developers in the world. Of those, 11.6 million were full-time developers and 6.4 million were part-time and nonprofessional developers.[25] It's not clear how the remaining developers are classified.

Now consider this: a 2015 SANS Institute State of Application Security Report explained, "Many information security engineers don't understand software development, and most software developers don't understand security."[26]

Of those programmers who actually went through a computer science program at a college or university, most of them never took a cybersecurity or secure coding course. Most self-taught programmers, who didn't receive any formal training, almost certainly lack any formal security training.

So, here's the first issue: there are millions of programmers who aren't familiar with, or don't understand, security and secure coding practices.

Now comes another major problem: when a company develops an application (app) and all the coding is done, they want to get it out as quickly as possible, so they can start making money. Most of the time an app's development starts without considering security. By the time the app is "ready" to put on the market, it should have gone through some testing and bug fixes. However, most apps will have had little, if any, real security testing performed on them. "Coders will, of course, make a due-diligence effort to flush out security flaws, but their main concerns are always more basic: They have to ship their product on time and ensure that it does what it's supposed to do."[27]

The reality is, trying to bolt security on at the end of development increases costs and time. It's more difficult to make an app secure when its development is done, or even almost finished, than it is to begin development with security at the forefront.

What's the bottom line? The U.S. Department of Homeland Security issued a software assurance report that estimates "90 percent of reported security incidents result from exploits against defects in the design or code of software."[28] With 2 billion lines of code being developed each week—by those who have little or no secure coding experience—there is a lot of room for security flaws.

Anti-malware

One of the biggest steps towards protecting your device from malware is to have an up-to-date anti-malware product installed on it. We mentioned anti-malware in an earlier chapter, and now we'll go a little more in depth.

Generically, anti-malware products are referred to as an antivirus. Rather than a single application, most anti-malware products are sometimes called solutions, as they incorporate various forms of anti-malware programs.

The most basic function of anti-malware is to scan your computer for and identify potential malware. In many cases, particularly for known malware, the infected file is deleted by the anti-malware.

Because of potential false positives, where the application flags a valid program or process as malware, the anti-malware may first quarantine potential malware. The quarantine allows the user to decide whether the identified malware is actually a valid process or not.

Several years ago, the anti-malware solution used by the organization I worked for flagged a valid Windows process as malware. In some cases, the process was actually deleted, which led to mass chaos because Windows computers began freezing and shutting down all over the campus. Many of those in IT thought we were under attack by some aggressive worm.

One of my machines had its antivirus update scheduled for the end of the day, instead of the beginning like most machines. That machine never got "infected," and I was able to research the issue. Some forums were reporting the same problem we were experiencing and had discovered it to be a false positive from the antivirus. At the time I was a fairly new technician, and when I mentioned what I discovered to one of the senior techs, I was ignored. Maybe there was more excitement about being under attack by a fast-moving worm than a simple false positive.

By late morning, the IT department learned from the vendor what was happening. Around lunchtime, the vendor issued an update, but the damage was done. For most "infected" computers, the solution was to copy the system file from a non-infected machine and replace the file that was deleted on the infected machine. For the few machines that had only quarantined the detected file, the file only needed to be released from quarantine for the machine to work normally.

Other services that an anti-malware solution might provide include adware blocker, anti-spyware, anti-phishing, or web browser plug-ins to help block malicious websites, advertisements, or network traffic.

Some anti-malware will simply scan for malicious files, comparing the scan to a directory of known malware known as signatures. Other anti-malware may incorporate a type of behavioral analysis, such as performing heuristic analysis on code.

Because the traditional, signature-based detection relies on previously identified malware, new variants of the same malicious code that change and adapt can be missed by these simple scans.

In a static heuristic analysis, the properties of the code are examined for suspicious characteristics, comparing those properties to various malware samples. If a specified percentage is matched, the file is identified as a potential threat.

In behavior-based detection, which is a form of dynamic analysis, the anti-malware examines how something behaves, usually by looking at the intended actions. Any attempted action that is abnormal or unauthorized is flagged as either suspicious or malicious.

If one's good, more must be better, right?

In my experience, I have seen some users run multiple (usually two, sometimes three or more) antivirus programs at the same time, reasoning that more would be better at catching malware.

The problem in running multiple anti-malware solutions (particularly from different developers/vendors) is, there is a possibility of a conflict among the differing antiviruses. More than one running anti-malware application also tends to decrease your computer's performance.

For those who want more than one antivirus, my recommendation is to have one main anti-malware solution running all the time. That means the anti-malware solution is regularly (at least daily) getting updates and performing regular system scans.

In addition, an on-demand anti-malware application can also be installed but not actively running. At least once a month, the user can manually launch this second application, update it, and scan the system.

Because rankings for anti-malware solutions vary from year to year, even among the different organizations ranking them, I won't go into specific applications.

On enterprise systems and personal computers, I have seen some paid anti-malware solutions clutter a computer, slow it down, and be less effective than some free anti-malware software. I've also seen plenty of free anti-malware products that slowed down the computer—and some that almost acted like malware. (It wasn't mentioned earlier, but there are even types of malware which pretend to be antivirus programs.)

With our organization, a previous vendor's product did well enough, but it frequently had complaints from the technicians. When the enterprise moved to a new solution a few years ago, from a new vendor, the change was noticeable. The new product detected much more than the previous solution, and calls for my help dealing with infected machines have dropped dramatically. I have to be careful with the new product because it has detected certain programs I have for my cybersecurity classes and deleted them—a problem I didn't have with the previous anti-malware product.

How does malware get on the device?

According to the 2018 Verizon Data Breach Investigations Report (DBIR), of 58,987,788 detected malware, the most common path to infection was through email, at 92.4 percent. Malware also infected devices from malicious websites or ads 6.3 percent of the time. Only 1.3 percent of infections were from other sources.[22]

It's not uncommon for a malware infection to come in two stages. The first-stage malware is what gets installed, often by the user. The malware then installs second-stage malware. Infected Javascript (.js), Visual Basic Script (.vbs), Microsoft Office, and PDF files are among the more common first-stage malware carriers. Windows executable (.exe) files are the most common second-stage malware.

The DBIR reports the frequency of malware file types as shown in the following table.

Table 2: Frequency of malware types, from DBIR report.

File Type	Frequency
.js	37.2%
.vbs	20.8%
Windows executable	14.8%
MS Office	14.4%
Other	7.0%
PDF	3.3%

Securing against malware

Here are some tips to keep your system more secure and your data protected—you'll notice some familiar ones:

- Keep your operating system updated.
- Keep your software applications updated.
- Keep your anti-malware (antivirus) updated and running.
- Download and install applications from approved sources.
- Be suspicious of links in your email, especially in unexpected messages.

We've already talked about the importance of keeping the operating system, applications, and anti-malware up-to-date.

What a lot of people don't realize is how much malware is associated with free downloads, especially from questionable sources. The reality is, it's difficult to know if the software you get is safe.

Maybe you're looking for a particular application, and, instead of going to an official site, you download the program from some other source. The program itself may be legitimate, but it might also have other programs installed with it.

Microsoft, Apple, and Google have attempted to help you by recommending that software applications only be obtained from approved "stores" like the Microsoft Store, the Apple Store, and Google Play Store. Many operating systems also have features that only allow approved software to be installed. Of course, those features can be overridden, but doing that puts your device at greater risk.

However, malicious applications have been found in manufacturer-approved stores. Even Apple's App Store has had malicious apps that collected user data and sent it to developer's server, some of which appear to be in China.[30]

We're used to clicking on links and going to a webpage. But, clicking on a link can also download a program onto your device. Depending on the system settings, it may even launch installation of the program, without you being aware of it.

Be extremely cautious of clicking on links in any email, and definitely don't click on links in any unexpected or suspicious email. We'll talk about phishing attacks in Chapter 8.

CHAPTER 8

Social Engineering

Social engineering is using human psychology to manipulate people into doing something they may not have done otherwise.

While social engineering is common in the virtual world, where it can be difficult to verify the true identify of an individual, social engineering also happens in the real world. An example might be someone posing as a technical support or delivery person and convincing the front desk to let them pass.

Social engineering is at the forefront of cybercrime. Within social engineering attacks, 91 percent start with an email.

When cybercriminals employ social engineering methods, they use social tactics to coax their victims into revealing confidential or sensitive information. Instead of spending months developing malware to access a system, social engineering attempts to trick people into freely giving up information, often their account information.

Common social engineering techniques

Many social engineering techniques use some form of psychological manipulation or trust exploitation.

Some social engineering tactics exploit our desire to be helpful. The attacker may pretend to be a coworker needing assistance. Or, the caller might say he's from human resources, and he needs you to log in to a new HR portal to approve your benefit package. Maybe the person is from the help desk, trying to find someone who called needing assistance.

Other tactics may exploit our fear. This could be fear of losing something, such being locked out of an account if you don't acknowledge the change by logging in.

Social engineering uses many methods. Some of the more common methods include

- phishing,
- spear phishing,
- vishing,
- pretexting,
- baiting,
- scareware, and
- access tailgating.

Some of these attack techniques are simple and easy to recognize. Others require the attacker to put in more work, but can have a huge payoff for the attacker because the attack may be harder to spot. In these methods, the attacker will investigate the target, identify potential victims, gather information, and determine possible attacks methods.

After laying the groundwork, the next step is the attempt to deceive the victim. The attacker will engage the target and will likely tell some story to legitimize the encounter. Because the attacker is prepared, the story may be very convincing.

The attacker's goal is to access as many systems as possible to get the most data. After seizing a little access, the attacker will attempt to expand the foothold in the organization. Data will be stolen wherever possible.

Ideally the attacker will try to leave without raising suspicion or tripping alerts. Any malware used will likely be removed when the job is done.

Access logs will be modified, if possible, and systems will be restored to a normal-looking state.

Phishing

Phishing is the most common form of social engineering. In its most basic form, a phishing attack is disguised to look like contact from a trusted source.

A phishing email tries to disguise itself as being from a legitimate source with the intent to deceive the recipient into giving away access information. The phishing email itself may be sent from a legitimate (although hacked or stolen) email address. Or it can be sent with a spoofed address, where the sender's address looks legitimate, but it's actually from another address.

Spam emails are sometimes confused with phishing emails, and there are a lot of similarities. Spam is unwanted email whose purpose is to get you to buy an advertised product. Spam is often sent by computers infected by certain kinds of malware. This malware turns the computer into a drone or zombie—a bot—which will then send more spam, usually from a legitimate email address. Many links and attachments in spam are malicious.

In 2017, phishing and pretexting were 98 percent of the social engineering incidents and the cause of 93 percent of breaches resulting from those incidents. Phishing alone grew by 65 percent from the previous year. These statistics only include incidents involving organizations and don't include attacks on customers.

The most common phishing attack method, at 96 percent, is through email. Of the 1,450 incidents reported in 2017, 381 had confirmed data breaches. Financial motivation occurred in 59 percent of those breaches, and 41 percent involved espionage.[31] A report from IBM found that 29 percent of all attacks on companies involved compromises through phishing emails.[32] The same report found nearly 40 percent of spam is estimated to originate from China.[33]

Verizon's 2018 Data Breach Investigations Report (DBIR) identified only 4 percent of users might click on phishing-related links, but those same users are more likely to fall for another phishing scam. Fifteen percent of those users will end up being successfully phished at least once more within the same year.

After a successful phishing attack, the attacker often follows up with malware installation and other attempts to obtain data.

The biggest thing to know is legitimate organizations will not ask you to verify your login credentials or ask for account information through an email link.

Here are some of the signs of a phishing attack:

- grammar and spelling mistakes
- non-personalized email, such as "Dear valued bank member"
- requests for personal or account information
- a sense of urgency, trying to get you to act quickly
- motivation for you to act out of fear, such as to confirm your credentials or you'll lose access to an account

While most phishing messages have a link, some phishing (and spam) emails have their message as an image. Attackers try to get around spam filters by disguising the text as an image, and often the image is the link. This can be revealed by moving the mouse over the "text," and the mouse pointer will change.

Attackers can easily find official company logos and information to make an email look authentic, so don't be fooled by official-looking emails.

To avoid being the victim of a phishing attack, carefully check all email links before clicking on them. Just because the link says it goes to a legitimate source doesn't mean it does. Links are frequently renamed to a friendly format. So, instead of having the full http:// address, the text might say "click here."

To check email links, hover your mouse over—but don't click on—the links to see where they actually go. This is most easily accomplished on a web browser or email client application. A web browser or email client application is better than a mobile device for viewing emails because although viewing email on a mobile device is convenient, seeing important information that can give away phishy email can be harder.

The following are actual emails I received while working at Utah Valley University (UVU). A few things to note:

- The "From" email did not originate from UVU. A mobile email viewer usually only displays the name and not the actual "From" address.
- The "To" address in one email is from some helpdesk.org and not the organization.
- The "Click Here" link goes to owaonlinks.myartsonline.com; most people would only pay attention to the beginning, which looks somewhat similar to the Outlook Web Application (OWA) site address that many organizations use for web email.

From: Mona Bamburg <mbamburg@nat.k12.la.us>
Date: January 14, 2015 at 4:47:02 PM MST
To: <info@helpdesk.org>
Subject: helpdesk

You have exceeded the storage limit set by your administrator; you will not be able to receive new mails until you upgrade your mailbox portal. To Upgrade - > Click Here:

Thanks,
System Administrator.

Figure 7: An actual phishing email I received when working at Utah Valley University.

The link in the next phishing email displays a link to what was at the time the actual login page. But, hovering over the link shows a completely different site that the link goes to. UVU is one of eight colleges and universities that are part of the Utah State Higher Education (USHE). Many employees are familiar with "USHE," so the "ushesite.net" link may not appear too suspicious. Interestingly, the site is also an "https," or secure site, which may also lower someone's suspicions.

Subject: Check Your Account

We have detected an increase in suspicious network activity and attempts to compromise in account to verify that your passwo https://ushesite.net/uvu/uvlink.uvu.edu/ ice any suspicious actr
Click to follow link

https://uvlink.uvu.edu/cp/home/displaylogin

Thank You.

Office of Information Technology

Figure 8: Another actual phishing email received.

The next email is a close-up of a web link, with the web address the link goes to. Besides the link going to a non-UVU site, the .ml site is the country domain code for Mali. I'm not sure why the IT Help Desk for UVU would have a link to a site with the Mali country code. You can easily do an internet search for these domains, which are referred to as a top-level domain.

Incidentally, most users weren't aware of it at the time, but UVU's help desk had been renamed "Service Desk" several months before I received this email, so any email signed as "Help Desk" was a phishing giveaway.

> http://edunation.ml/includes/update/page2/
> **Click to follow link**

IT Service Support. Click Here to validate Email to 2016 webmail now.

Thank you
IT Help Desk

Figure 9: Hovering your mouse (not clicking) over a link shows where the link will actually go.

Pay close attention to—but don't click on—the links. Examine the entire address, not just the first part. A change in characters can easily appear like a legitimate website, as our brains automatically want to correct errors. Longer addresses can easily betray your mind into thinking they're good sites. Beware of legitimate-sounding names but different domains, such as a "cn" or "co" instead of "com." Here are some examples:

Table 3: Legitimate sites compared to phishy sites.

Legitimate Site	Phishy Sites
www.microsoft.com	www.mircosoft.com
	www.micosoft.com
www.google.com	www.goog1e.com
www.bankofamerica.com	www.bankofarnerica.com
	www.bankofamerca.com
www.amazon.com	www.amaz0n.com
www.yahoo.com	www.yah00.com
support.microsoft.com	support.microsoft.corn.co

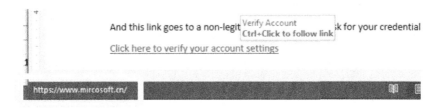

Figure 10: A link I created in Microsoft Word.

The following are a few examples to get you to act now, before you have a chance to really consider if the email is valid or not. Remember, the goal is for you to act quickly, often out of fear or convenience. These are from actual phishing emails.

- "For security reasons, you are required to secure and revalidate your mailbox."
- "Part of our duty is to strengthen the security of your mailbox. Please login to make sure you are familiar with the new settings."
- "Your mailbox is nearly full. Please increase your mailbox quota size by clicking HERE."
- "Your account will be disabled today because it is outdated and has not been upgraded to include the latest security features."
- "Failure to do this will have your account suspended."
- "Your password expires in 3 days."
- "Fill out the requirements to automatically revalidate your mailbox and upgrade its quota size."

On the next pages are several real phishing examples, along with the web pages their links would go to.

Thu 4/17/2014 8:21 PM

Urata, Richard Atsuki. (ARC-SST)[OAK RIDGE ASSOCIATE

RE:

To   Urata, Richard Atsuki. (ARC-SST)[OAK RIDGE ASSOCIATED UNIVERSITIES (ORAU)]

From: Urata, Richard Atsuki. (ARC-SST)[OAK RIDGE ASSOCIATED UNIVERSITIES (ORAU)]
Sent: Thursday, April 17, 2014 7:00 PM
To: Urata, Richard Atsuki. (ARC-SST)[OAK RIDGE ASSOCIATED UNIVERSITIES (ORAU)]
Subject:

We want to upgrade all email account scheduled for today as part of our duty to strengthen security of your mailbox. CLICK HERE to upgrade your account to Outlook Web Apps 2014. If your settings is not updated today, your account will be inactive and cannot send or receive message any longer.
Sincerely,
IT Helpdesk.

Figure 11: A phishing email. Note the appeal for your help to "strengthen security" and the sense of urgency to act now, or your account will become inactive.. Like many phishing emails, the English grammar is a bit lacking.

IF YOU KNOW YOUR EMAIL IS STILL VALID.FILL THE NECCESSSARY DETAILS
ON THE FORM AND WRITE REPORT NOTE::

E-MAIL VERIFICATION

E-MAIL:::::::::

USER NAME:::::::::

PASSWORD:::::::::::

CONFIRM PASSWORD:::::::::

WORK SINCE:::::::::

SEND TO VERIFY

Figure 12: The website the phishing link, from the previous figure, will take you to.

From: "Garcia, ███████████ 3@sru.edu>
Date: April 28, 2014 at 5:07:45 AM MDT
To: "employeedesk@webmaster.edu" <employeedesk@webmaster.edu>
Subject: SUSPECT: General web-mail maintenance

General web-mail maintenance
Dear Account Owner,
We want to upgrade all Microsoft Exchange email account scheduled for today as part of our duty to strengthen security of your mailbox. CLICK HERE<http://www.soundipod.com/smtpupgrade/> to upgrade your account to Outlook Web Apps 2014. If your settings is not updated today, your account will be inactive and cannot send or receive message any longer.
Sincerely,
-IT Department
Microsoft Corporation. All rights reserved

Figure 13: Another phishing email. Note the "From" and "To" emails. The "To" email is likely legitimate, but what about "webmaster.edu?" The From email uses common words, "employeedesk" (like employee help desk) and "webmaster," hoping your mind will recognize them and not pay attention to the detail. If this From email were legitimate, then there would be an educational institution called Webmaster. Maybe it's a college for web developers. This email also showcases lack of grammar.

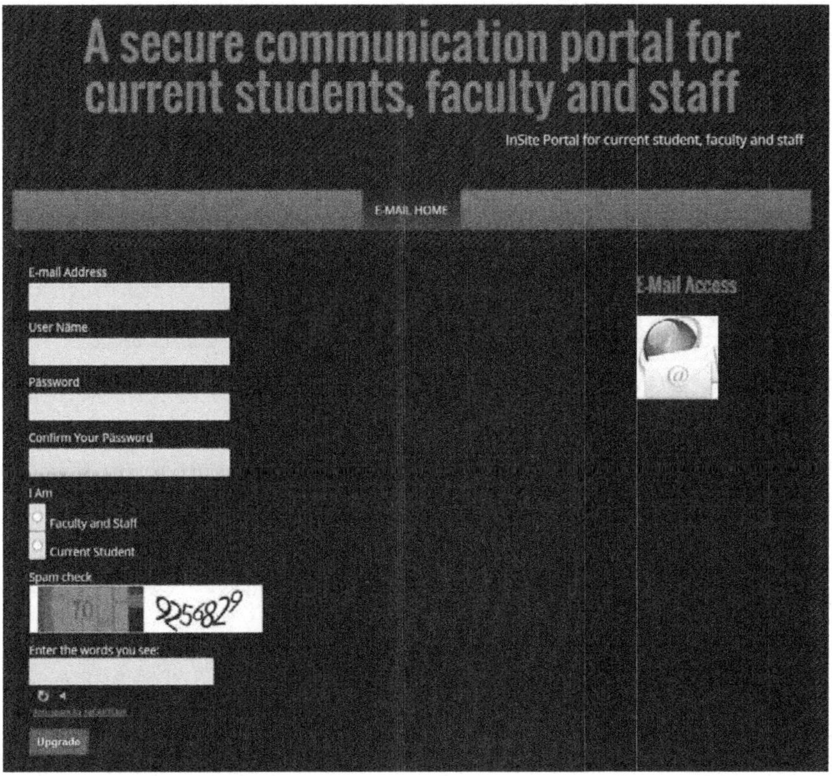

Figure 14: The login site for the previous phishing email. Note the attempt to look official, with "spam check" and the Captcha images, where you're asked to enter the words from the images.

From: Param█████████nan [mailto:p██████ry@nre.gov.my]
Sent: Saturday, February 15, 2014 12:42 PM
Subject: Read: Service Help-desk

Attention E-mail Owner,

IMPORTANT WARNING MESSAGE FROM THE WEB-MAIL ADMIN
TEAM, A 2014 DFXG Virus has been detected on your mail and your
account will be terminated in a short time from our database.Please click on the
below link or copy and lo-gin your full email address for maintenance
and Virus Scanning, Very Important.

http://e-mailadminiistratorsserver14.hexat.com/index

Thanks for your understanding and Co-operation.

System Management Team,
© Copyright 2014

Figure 15: Another phishing email, this one uses the threat of a virus on your system.

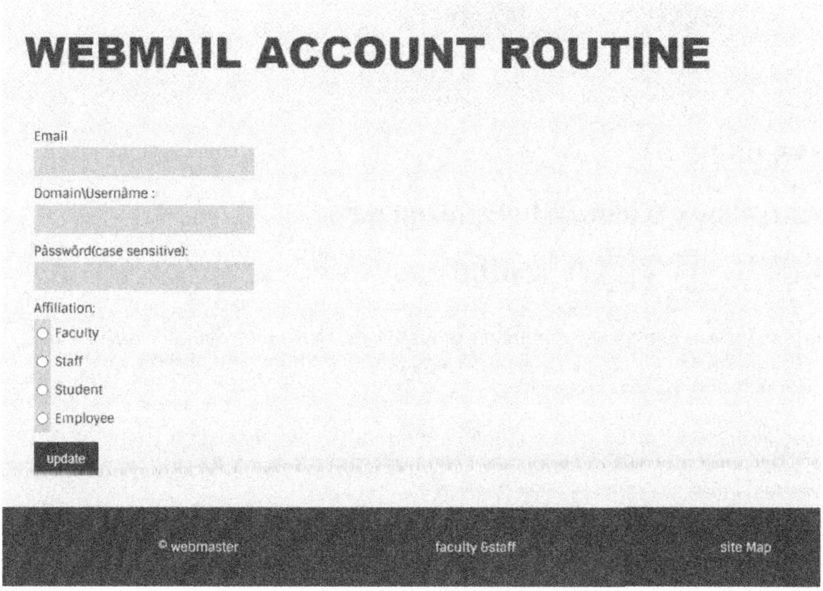

WEBMAIL ACCOUNT ROUTINE

Email

Domain\Username :

Pàsswôrd(case sensitive):

Affiliation:
- ○ Faculty
- ○ Staff
- ○ Student
- ○ Employee

update

© webmaster   faculty &staff   site Map

Figure 16: The login website from the previous phishing email.

From: Wayne █████ [mailto:wayne█████@snow.edu]
Sent: Monday, February 17, 2014 7:07 AM
To: Wayne Squire
Subject: ADMIN TEAM (URGENT NOTIFICATION).

DEAR USER,

Your mailbox is almost full and out dated.

1.93GB	**2.01GB**

This is to inform you as our webmail account User, that our webmail Admin server provider is currently congested, and your Mailbox is out of date. so we are deleting inactive accounts.

Please verify your webmail account by automatically by clicking on ITS HELPDESK and fill-out the necessary requirements to automatically verify and increase your mailbox quota size.

IMPORTANT NOTE: You won't be able to send and receive mail messages at 1.97GB.

ITS help desk
ADMIN TEAM

©Copyright 2014 Microsoft, Inc.
All Rights Reserved

Figure 17: A phishing email using a sense of urgency to keep your webmail from being deleted.

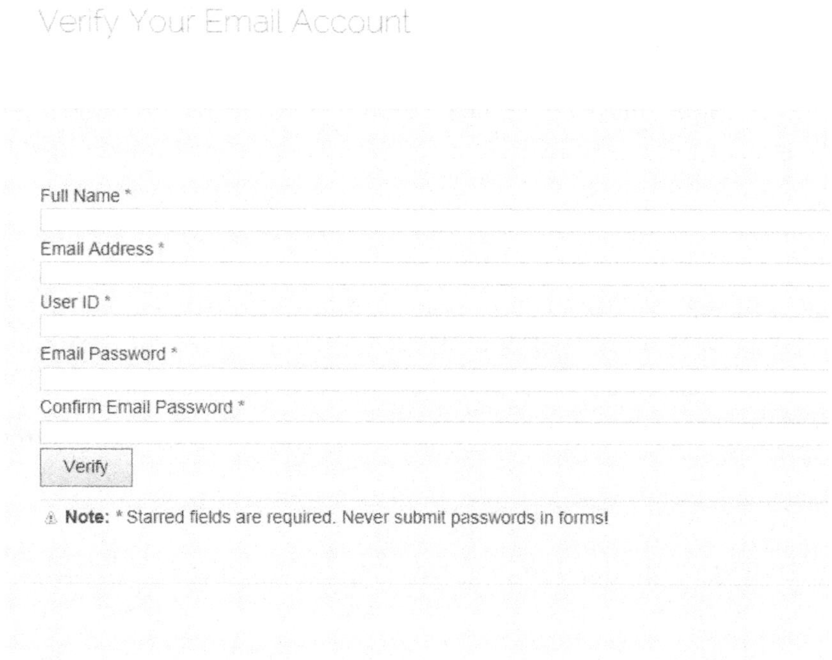

Verify Your Email Account

Full Name *

Email Address *

User ID *

Email Password *

Confirm Email Password *

[Verify]

⚠ **Note:** * Starred fields are required. Never submit passwords in forms!

Figure 18: Here's the website login for the previous email. I thought the "Never submit passwords in forms!" notice was a nice touch.

Spear phishing

Spear phishing is almost identical to phishing, except the email is customized to target a specific individual or organization.

Vishing

Vishing, also called voice phishing, is "the use of social engineering over the phone to gather personal and financial information from the target."[34]

One vishing tactic would be to call the front desk, or someone listed in the online company directory, and use some pretext to get certain information.

To avoid being a victim of vishing, be careful not to provide or confirm any personal or financial information if you get an unexpected call. If you're concerned about the issue—maybe you get a call about some credit card fraud and you're asked to verify your credit card number—hang up and call a legitimate number, not one provided to you by the caller.

In my experience, most calls I have received about potential credit card fraud (usually because I was out of state and making abnormal purchases) were automated calls. These calls basically asked to confirm whether the card was used or not. The full card number was never read over the phone, nor was it ever asked for.

Pretexting

Pretexting is where the scammer makes up some scenario and pretends to need certain information from you, such as to confirm your identity. Instead of using fear and urgency to motivate, the pretext often tries to foster a false sense of trust.

The difference between pretexting and phishing is that pretexting lacks reliance on malware. Pretexting is generally more about getting information directly from the target, and it is financially motivated 95 percent of the time.[35] Pretexting can be useful in getting information to use in a phishing, or spear-phishing, attack.

Financial pretexting incidents rose from 61 incidents in 2016 to 170 incidents in 2017, with the largest increase targeting human resources staff.

I recently received a call from someone claiming to be from a major national sweepstakes. The caller claimed to be the driver delivering the prize and was wondering if I was home. When I told him I wasn't and my wife was, I was directed to call the manager to arrange the prize delivery. I was too busy to play the game, otherwise I might have called the "manager." A little while later, the "driver" called to see if I had contacted the manager. When I replied that I had been too busy, the driver immediately hung up, sounding, I might add, frustrated that he'd wasted his time.

In this case, the false pretense was that I'd won the sweepstakes. The call was unexpected, and the news was surprising—something most people only dream of. Such unbelievable news is enough to throw somebody off guard. That's the goal: catch the victim off guard so they will make a mistake. In this case, the attempt would've been to string the victim (me) along, making me believe I was about to get millions. I probably would've had to provide bank information at some point. If I'd played along, it would likely have become a sweepstakes scam, which is mentioned later.

Baiting

Baiting can be similar to phishing attacks, but in baiting, the attacker uses an offer, such as free music or a free download, to get users to give up login credentials. Or, instead of giving up login credentials, the offered free download may have malicious software attached to it.

Baiting can also involve the use of a physical object. One method is for criminals to infect USB thumb drives with malware, then leave the drives in public areas, like a parking lot. If the hackers are targeting a specific organization, they may leave the drives around that facility.

The strategy relies on human curiosity. While some people will pick up a drive to find the owner, others will be curious as to what's on it. Others will keep the drive as their own. In any case, the goal is for someone to put the drive in their computer.

Those who plug the USB drive in to their device risk malware infection. If the anti-malware doesn't catch the malware, your device may become compromised.

Your best course of action when you find an unknown USB drive is to not plug it in to your computer but turn it in to the lost-and-found.

Quid pro quo

This attack is similar to baiting, except the quid pro quo offer is usually for a service.

Quid pro quo attacks work because they're based on reciprocity. If someone does something nice for us, we feel obligated to return the favor.

A common quid pro quo attack comes when an attacker assumes the guise of IT support calling back in response to a request for help. The attacker may call various numbers within an organization and will often find somebody who needs IT help.

Having worked as an IT technician for a long time, I can tell you this would probably work really well. There are less than 50 people in the department I primarily serve. If I walk through the department, it is fairly common somebody will ask me a tech question or need help with something they've been meaning to ask me about.

If someone were to start randomly calling a bunch of people in an organization, claiming to be responding to an IT request, there's a high chance the attacker will successfully find someone needing help. Using the trust that people tend to give to IT support, the attacker may be able to convince the person to disable an anti-malware product and install a software "update" to help fix the problem.

Way back in 2003, an unscientific survey by Infosecurity Europe found that 90 percent of "office workers at London's Waterloo Station gave away their computer password for a cheap pen, compared with 65 percent"[36] the year before. The survey asked a variety of questions, and 75 percent of those who were asked "What is your password?" actually gave their password. The other 15 percent, who initially refused to give up their password, ended up revealing their password after some social engineering tricks. One person who refused said, "I am the CEO, I will not give you my password—it could compromise my company's information." After a few more questions, the CEO mentioned that his daughter's name was his password. The interviewer then asked, "What's your daughter's name?" and, without thinking, the CEO told him the name.

It'd be nice to think more people are more security conscious now than back in 2003, but it may not be the case.

In 2016, the University of Luxembourg conducted a study with 1,208 randomly selected passersby who were asked questions about their attitude towards computer security.[37] The interviewers had a University of Luxembourg bag but were unknown to those they interviewed. The interviewers gave some people a chocolate bar before the interview and gave some people the chocolate bar after the interview. The study showed that the small gift of a chocolate bar before the interview versus after increased the chances of participants revealing their password.

Of the participants given chocolate before the interview, 43.5 percent shared their passwords. That percentage increased to 47.9 percent if the chocolate was given immediately before the person was asked to share their password. On the other hand, of the participants who were given chocolate after the interview, 29.8 percent revealed their passwords.

While the percentage of those who revealed their passwords was less in 2016 than in 2003, there is still plenty of room for improvement. This is particularly true when 30 percent to almost 50 percent of people may be more willing to share their password if they're given a gift.

Scareware

This attack attempts to trick you into thinking your computer has a problem, such as being infected with malware, or that illegal content was downloaded. The warning may give you the option to have the problem fixed by calling a support number, or by downloading an "anti-virus" or other software than can fix the problem.

If you decide to click on the link to download the solution that will "fix" the problem, you may have to first pay for the program. After you've paid and installed the program, you'll see the problem (which was non-existent to start with) go away, and you may be impressed with how quickly the solution worked. So, when another problem comes up later, you might be offered another "solution" for another price.

If you call number, the person may offer to fix the problem for you. You may be required to pay for the support or for the application that will be installed on your machine.

In any case, you can be assured that the installed software is the actual malware.

My experience with scareware is it usually locks up the web browser and, in some cases, may even take over the screen, seeming to not allow the user to do anything else. Often, clicking the "X" to close the window probably won't work. Most users start to panic and believe their device is infected.

Since most of the users I work with have Microsoft Windows on their computers, the normal fix is to open the processes in Task Manager (the shortcut is the ctrl-shift-esc keys) and end the running application, which is usually the web browser. Then, web browser settings and internet options can be checked (or even reset) to clear any newly added home pages, search engines, cookies, and other web-related content. It doesn't happen often, but I have had users get "re-infected" with the scareware if the web browser settings were changed and not reset.

Access tailgating

In an access tailgating attack, also known as piggybacking, the goal is for someone without proper authentication to gain access into a restricted area. This attack exploits the goodness of most people being willing to help out.

Have you ever entered a door that required a proximity access card, or a code, to enter? Have you ever had a coworker or someone you were sure worked in another department hurry over or ask you to hold the door so they could enter without fumbling with their own card or entering the code? This is access tailgating, where someone enters a restricted area without using their own access permissions.

A common method is for someone to impersonate a delivery driver and wait until someone is about to enter the door. The delivery person then comes along with a big package and asks the employee to hold the door for them. With every intention of being helpful, the employee usually holds the door, and may even help, while the unauthorized person enters.

Tailgating may not even involve a proximity card or code. Maybe all that needs to happen is to pass the front desk person, whose job it is to keep unauthorized people from passing. The person may start a friendly conversation with the employee, demonstrating enough familiarity that the front desk lets them pass.

Most of us want to be helpful. However, the best defense is to make sure employees understand the importance of verifying the credentials and authorization of those you don't know before allowing them to pass a checkpoint.

Scams

In one way or another, the goal of many social engineering attacks is to con you out of money or information. Scams are social engineering that are like malware targeting the person. These scams come through social media, email, your phone, and even in person. Scams happen both in the real world and online, and we'll go over some examples in a bit.

Like a phishing attack, a scam may seem legitimate. Sometimes the scam manipulates your good emotions. Other scams may threaten you with arrest, fines, or something else. Scammers want to knock you off guard so you forget to use common sense. Almost always, the scam will be urgent and employ some kind of motivator to get you to act quickly without thinking about it.

Scammers trying to defraud you out of money will usually request the money be sent through some non-recoverable means. These payments might be gift cards, reloadable credit cards, wire transfers, and sometimes through a payment app on a phone or computer. If the gift card or reloadable credit card is requested, the scammer may just want the card's number given to them.

Here are some of the common scams. Several of them have primarily been phone scams, but the internet is expanding the scams to an online presence.

Virtual kidnapping scam

It's a call feared by parents. You answer your phone and a girl's crying voice is heard briefly, "Sorry daddy," and then a man gets on the line and tells you he's kidnapped your daughter. To save her life, you're told to comply with some instructions—stay on the phone, don't contact anyone else, and send a ransom. Of course, the ransom money will probably need to be sent using a non-recoverable wire transfer.

How does this scam get pulled off? The scammer usually gets information from social media. They find out names, ages, schools, and other information to make it sound legitimate. But, a simple phone call—even if you need to write a note asking someone else to make the call for you—can discover the truth.

A comment about the "ransom," "fee," or other money you may be asked to pay. Often the amount is less than a few thousand, which is substantial for most of us. However, the amount is small enough it's often not worth the time and cost for the FBI and other law enforcement agencies to chase after. But, if the crime can be linked with others, then it can become a higher value investigation.

Grandparent/family emergency scam

These scams usually target the elderly, with the scammer often pretending to be a grandchild in trouble. Usually the scammer has gotten information from a social media site, which he uses to make the scam sound more legitimate and fool the victim. After the victim is convinced, which can happen quickly, the urgent situation is explained. Maybe the "grandchild" is in jail and needs bail money or there's a medical emergency. In any case, the situation is urgent and money is needed right away.

If you receive this type of communication, make sure you verify the situation first by calling the grandchild directly or talking to another family member. If the scammer wants to keep the conversation secret, that's usually a big red flag it's a scam.

IRS scam

The caller/emailer/texter claims to be from the IRS, calling with regards to outstanding taxes, and, usually, threatens severe action if the taxes aren't paid. The threats may include arrest, license suspension, or deportation (if the caller suspects the victim might be an "illegal" immigrant). The caller demands that payment be made with very short notice, usually that day.

The IRS will never contact an individual by phone, email, or text or demand payment on short notice. If someone is delinquent on taxes they usually receive notice of the delinquency through regular mail. If you have questions, call the IRS.

Additional tax scams and related alerts can be found at https://www.irs.gov/newsroom/tax-scams-consumer-alerts.

Jury duty scam

The call usually comes from someone claiming to be a US Marshal or other law enforcement agent, threatening you for missing jury duty. They may give you a badge number, and the phone number might be spoofed to appear local, all to fool you into thinking the call is legitimate. Usually you'll be told you can avoid prosecution and potential jail time by paying a fine, which you're given very short notice to pay. Like other scams, payment is often preferred by gift card, reloadable credit card, or wire transfer.

No government entity would threaten you with arrest over the phone.

Romance scam

These scams are mostly online and usually through a social media or dating site. The scammer creates a fraudulent profile. Sometimes the scammer may claim to be in the military or away on a business trip.

A big difference with this type of scam is it often takes days or weeks of correspondence. The scammer works to build up rapport and trust with their victim. Once trust is established, the scammer will ask for money. Maybe it's for a ticket to see the victim or there's some financial hardship. Like other scams, money is requested via difficult-to-recover methods.

Another romance scam tactic is the scammer may threaten to publicize sensitive information you sent them (photos, messages, etc.). Of course, they claim that if you pay them, they won't go through with the blackmail—until the next time they want to extort money from you.

In another variation, the scammer may contact you and claim the person you have been messaging was a minor and threaten to call law enforcement unless you immediately pay them.

Tech support scams

Tech support scams were touched on earlier, where the scammer pretends to be technical support for some company, like Microsoft or Apple. They may claim to have detected a problem on your computer. There are several tactics the scammer might use. Some will ask for payment for the service. Most will want to remotely access the computer. Once they have access to the device, they'll look for personal information, install malware, or lock the victim out of the computer and demand payment to unlock it.

"Suspended" Social Security numbers

In this type of scam, you receive notice, most likely by phone, that your Social Security number is suspended. The caller informs you that due to fraud or other illegal activity, your number has been "suspended." To "reactivate" your number, you just need to verify, by providing the caller with, your personal information.

In case you're wondering, Social Security numbers don't get suspended.

Fraudulent online offers and sales

These scams are the number one complaint to consumer protection agencies. They include product misrepresentations, deceptive practices, unauthorized charges, and non-disclosed re-stocking fees.

If an offer sounds too good to be true, it probably is.

Sweepstakes and lotteries

These scams are among the more prevalent in the county. Scammers may pretend to be affiliated with a well-known organization, or they may give the name of a non-existent one. Victims are informed of their winnings, but they need to pay "taxes" or a "delivery fee" first.

Individuals, under Federal Law, are not required to pay any amount up front—for any reason—before collecting legitimate winnings.

Payments are requested in the usual ways for scams. Occasionally, the scammer may give you a fake check to cover the costs. You'll be asked to deposit the check and wire transfer the extra back. The scammer hopes you'll wire the money before the check bounces.

Earlier I shared my experience with a caller claiming to be the delivery driver for a major sweepstakes I'd supposedly won. The scam began as a pretext.

Credit reports and repair

There are a lot of credit repair companies claiming to fix negative information and bad credit. But, only time and effort can correct bad credit. Don't get fooled into paying for a credit report when you can get one free.

One free credit report can be obtained each year from each of the three credit reporting bureaus. Spaced out, you could get three reports each year, one from each agency. They will also, for a small fee, provide you a copy of your report.

Advance fee loans

The scammer represents himself as legitimate lender who can secure loans for those with little or bad credit. An upfront fee, sometimes referred to as a processing fee, application fee, or "credit insurance," is required.

Legitimate companies may charge fees for their services, but reputable companies deduct these fees from the costs of the loan or the fee is only required if the loan is approved.

Typical targets for these scams are those who may have already applied for high-interest, short-term loans. Here are some warning signs for these scams:

- A promise of a "guaranteed" loan—watch out for individuals promising a loan without a credit check. Legitimate lenders have minimum credit requirements and will have a credit check before approving the loan.
- Loans offered over the phone—if a company is doing business solely over a phone with an individual, it is against federal law to promise a loan or credit card and ask for payment before the loan or card is delivered.
- If you're asked to use a delivery service other than USPS, the scammer may be trying to avoid federal postal inspectors and avoid charges of mail fraud.
- Out-of-state lenders, which makes it difficult to gather information about the company and can make prosecution more challenging.
- Non-registered lenders—lenders conducting business are to be registered in the state.

Work-at-home schemes

These schemes are all over the internet. While there are some legitimate work-at-home businesses, advertisements promising high income for limited effort are scams. Common "jobs" include envelope stuffing, craft assembly, rebate processing, and mystery shopping.

When I was earning my first bachelor's degree, I fell for an envelope-stuffing scam, but back then the job was posted as an ad in the paper. I was looking for a way to make additional income and sent some money (I think it was $20) to get information on how to earn money stuffing envelopes. I was disappointed with myself for falling for what ended up being a scam. There may be different versions of the scam, but this is what I remember about this one.

For my $20, I received an envelope with instructions to set up a PO Box and to place ads in papers about earning money stuffing envelopes (if I remember right, the instructions even had a few examples of ads). When I received a reply with the $20 fee, I was instructed to send the person a copy of the instructions. I never did it. I learned I was a classic victim. I was needing some more money, even feeling a little desperate, and fell for what looked like an easy way to get a little more money. I've since learned to be more suspicious.

Other scams and complaints

These other scams don't usually have a lot of technology behind them; that is, they don't usually come through email, texts, or phone calls. But, you need to be aware of them, as they can take your money and maybe even some of your personal information.

- retail—false advertising, defective products, product and price misrepresentation
- car purchases and repair—implied warranties when none exist, not getting express authorization for additional unforeseen but necessary repairs, inspections, or other services for amounts in excess of the legally established percentage about the original estimate
- coaching services—misrepresentation of services that are provided and the results of the program, as well as selling services for overpriced fees
- telemarketing—callers falsely presenting themselves as solicitors or representatives of a legitimate charity, business, or government agency
- charitable solicitations—unregistered solicitors not using solicited donations for the stated purpose
- direct solicitations—misrepresentations of services or for nonexistent affiliations. These include door-to-door sales
- alarm systems—aggressive sales tactics and misrepresentations in the door-to-door solicitations

Years ago, I worked as an installer for a security company. Most of the sales staff were generally honest. A couple salesmen were exceptional, and I liked installing their sales because the customers knew what to expect and were given thorough, accurate information before they agreed to the sale.

But, there were several on the sales team who were manipulative and aggressive in their approaches and were only trying to make sales. I disliked installing for them. Customers were usually over-promised, sometimes told about non-existent or over-exaggerated features, and I always had to re-sell the customer based on the actual capabilities of the system.

Those sales staff just wanted me to install and not ask questions. They liked me because I was a good, thorough installer, but they thought I'd end up losing their sale if I talked to the customer too much. I only lost one sale in all my re-selling efforts (the salesman wasn't happy).

The sales staff who liked me were the ones I also enjoyed installing for. They knew I'd work with the customer and make sure they were taken care of right.

A couple months into the job, I was tired of the unscrupulous sales tactics of the few and quit. The company pulled out of the area soon after and went bankrupt a few years later. The company had started out doing well, but I think the misrepresentations and dishonesty of some of their employees cost them the business.

Another area where scams and complaints occur is related to home improvement and repairs. These include overcharges, substandard work, and failure to even complete the job. To avoid problems, make sure you get the estimate in writing before any work starts—and be sure it includes the price estimate, summary of work and materials to be used, when the work will start, estimated completion date, responsibility for cleanup, and any applicable warranties or guarantees. Read and understand any paperwork before you sign it. And, don't forget to always get a receipt for any payment made.

Several years ago, we almost fell victim to a duct cleaning company's attempt to get more money from us. The cleaning process was started, and the technician informed us we needed some sanitizing of the system. While it was probably true, the extra service cost several hundred more dollars more than the cleaning price quoted. We got the ducts cleaned but declined the sanitation add-on. We did get the cleaning estimate in writing before the work had started, and while it was good to get the ducts cleaned, I wasn't impressed with the technician, who was a little careless.

Social media

Social media is a catch-all term for a variety of websites that build on the idea of traditional social networks, where you connect with other people. Typically, you set up a profile with information about yourself and then communicate with others through chat rooms, messaging, forums, etc.

While most users of social media sites are not a threat, these sites do attract those with malicious intent.

Those of us with children and youth need to be particularly mindful of what our children are doing online. Children under the age of 13 should not be using social media, and even teenagers need to be educated to the potential threats that exist from online predators.

These predators exploit those who are most vulnerable, especially children. Some are twisted in their perversions, and take advantage of, abuse, and do much worse to their victims. Others attempt to befriend and then, through fraud, force, or coercion, compel their victim into various forms of human trafficking, including sexual exploitation, drugs, and forced labor. Many victims are first ensnared in the predator's trap through social media contact.

It's not just youth who are vulnerable to social media scams. However, keep in mind that much of the following will apply to keeping kids safe as well.

Security implications

Because social media encourages the sharing of information, much of which is personal, people are often not as cautious online as they might be in a real-world setting. The feeling of anonymity and lack of actual physical interaction tends to provide a false sense of security to a lot of people. Most people share comments for their friends and forget that others might be able to view what they posted.

It's relatively easy to set up a social media account. There is little to prevent someone from creating a fake account and attempting to get you to accept a friend request or to get one of your friends to accept their friend request; through that request to you or your friend, they can possibly see your profile, and, through that, request possibly see your profile. The information obtained from a person's profile, including their comments, can be used in various social engineering attacks.

Once the attacker has access to your profile, they may discover information about where you live, what you do for work, what hobbies you enjoy. They may be able to impersonate a friend or family member.

It is unfortunate, but social media has become a tool scammers box of tricks. Besides posing as a grandchild, relative, or friend, the scammer may pose as a police officer, doctor, or lawyer. In any case, the scammer is usually after money or information and sometimes various forms of exploitation.

While these scams happen too frequently, a grandparent scam in early 2019 managed to convince a man, over several phone calls, to send over $80,000.[38] The man was convinced his grandson was in trouble. Thankfully the man's daughter contacted the police, and they were able to arrest three people in connection with the scam.

But fraud is all too common. There is a new trend where the scammer asks for cash to be mailed. At the end of 2018, the Federal Trade Commission reported that among all age groups, the median amount lost by individuals to imposters was about $2,000. "But the story is much worse for people 70 and over who sent cash — they reported median individual losses of $9,000."[39]

To help protect you from scams, keep these two basics in mind:

- No matter how dramatic or urgent the story, don't act right away.
- Call the person using a phone number you know is right—not one the caller gives you. If you can't reach the person, contact someone who might know. The caller may ask you to keep it a secret, but it's vital you know the truth.

Be careful with what you post on social media. The information may be used to defraud you or someone you care about.

Keeping safe on social media

Here are some recommendations for keeping safe on social media. Many of them are repeated elsewhere in this book.

Use a strong password for every social media site. Each social media account should have its own password.

Most sites require setting up security questions; make sure to set them up.

If the site offers two-factor authentication, opt in and set it up. Two-factor authentication can do more to keep your account safe than the security questions.

If you use a social media app on your phone, your phone should also have a password. Of course, your phone should have a password/code/etc. set up on it regardless of whether you have a social media app on it.

Be careful with friend requests. Too many people just want more "friends," even if they don't know the person making the request. If you don't know the person, it's safer to not accept the friend request, as it could be a fake account.

Be careful with what you share, and don't share too much. There is certain information you should not share about yourself or any members of your family. Never share

- date and place of birth,
- home address and phone number,
- credit card numbers,
- banking information,
- passwords, or
- Social Security numbers.

Be familiar with and adjust your privacy settings. Don't trust the default privacy settings to be set to protect your privacy. Often, defaults are set to make it easier to be social, by sharing everything. General privacy settings range from private, where nothing is shared, to public, where it's open to everyone. The more common settings are public (open to everyone), friends only (only visible to those whom you've accepted as friends), and friends of friends (which opens your profile information to anyone your friends have accepted as a friend). Some sites will allow you to create customized groups of friends or family. Often the different parts of your profile, including different photo albums and comments, can be set to have differing privacy settings.

Be cautious about setting anything to public. Public is exactly as it sounds. Nobody even needs to be a registered user of the social media site to see it, which means anyone can see it. For most social media, it's probably best to keep as much as possible limited to friends and family.

Don't share personal details. This also includes personal details about members of your family. If you have children, be extremely selective in what you share and with whom.

Social media sites encourage interaction, sharing memorable moments, and connecting with others. Especially for those who thrive on this type of sharing, it can be easy to reveal too much that can expose you, your family, or your home as an easy target.

It can be hard not to share an exciting experience you're having on a vacation. But wait until you are home from the vacation. Never share the information that you are away on vacation, shopping, or travelling. Wait until you're back home to share your experiences.

Also, never share when you are leaving or when you'll be home.

Information about when you are or will be gone from your home gives criminals a heads up when your house is empty and an easy target.

ABC News reported on October 2, 2018, that a string of burglaries of homes of celebrities left police in the Los Angeles area looking for clues in what appeared to be random occurrences. Some of the victims included well-known musicians, actors, producers, and professional athletes.

"Initially, it was believed that the homes were being burglarized at random. Detectives learned, however, that this wasn't the case. The victims' homes had been selected based on social media posting, touring or travel schedules of the owners."[40]

You might be thinking, "But I'm not a celebrity." Do you have anything of value in your home? Items of value include cash, jewelry, electronics, vehicles, credit cards, guns, and prescription drugs.

What about sensitive documents—financial information, birth certificates, identification cards, deeds, titles, or other documentation that could be used to commit fraud or identity theft? These documents might be hard copies or digital copies.

Most of us have something of value—and probably a lot more than you may realize.

Something else to consider: your social media posts might invalidate your homeowner's insurance in the case of a burglary.

While it may not be affecting the U.S. much, an August 2018 article in Britain's *The Telegraph* stated, "Insurers are increasingly rejecting claims made by customers whose houses have been burgled while on holiday if they have shared the fact that they are away from home on Facebook, Twitter or Instagram."[41]

The clause that exists in most policies is that homeowners are to take "reasonable care" in keeping their home and property safe. In some cases, insurers have determined that posting vacation photos and messages, while on vacation, is a breach of this clause.

Not every insurer will reject a claim based on social media posts, but enough are doing so that the British Financial Ombudsman and police issued the warning. Research by Admiral insurers found that one in 20 burglaries happened while the owners were on vacation, and another survey revealed "one in 12 Britons had been burgled after posting their location abroad on social media."[42]

An article on *ABC News* states that "78 percent of burglars are using social media to find their targets."[43]

If you use social media, here are a few more things to be aware of.

Limit access to work history

Résumés and detailed job histories are a treasure trove of information. Often, résumés can reveal a lot about one's personal life and even give useful information to hack the account or commit identity theft.

Anonymity—who are you really connecting with?

It's easy to set up a false account. Among other reasons, these accounts may be set up to

- make false statements about someone else,
- cause legal or personal problems or embarrass someone,
- send people to a malicious website, or
- commit fraud.

Before you accept a friend request, verify the identity of the person behind the account.

Unfortunately, law enforcement too frequently discovers a child predator who has set up a false account, often pretending to be a youth, in order to get to a minor.

But, it's not just youth and children who are targeted. Even adults are fooled by scammers on social media sites.

Take control of the comments

Just as false accounts can be set up and can cause problems, comments by impersonators can also cause issues. Be proactive in controlling comments on your profile. If your children have social media accounts, you should know what is on their accounts and be aware of the comments there.

Social engineering defense

Many of the following are similar to previously discussed defenses for social engineering attacks. These recommendations can keep your devices, you and your family, and your personal information better protected:

- Don't open emails from untrusted sources. If it's from an unfamiliar source, especially if it's unsolicited, just delete it.

- Be wary of emails that are unexpected or emails that are unlike those you normally receive from the sender. Emails get hacked, contact lists get stolen, and the cybercriminal will try to get you to open an email from a familiar address. But, if a friend or family member sends you an email that is unlike the normal ones you receive from them, contact them in person or by phone, and ask about the email.

- Beware of offers from strangers. Just as you probably learned from your parents to not talk with strangers, the same is true online. An offer that seems too good to be true probably is. The internet and social media make it easy for people to misrepresent their motives as well as their identities.

- Lock your computer and other devices when you are away from them. This doesn't mean a physical lock necessarily, but lock the screen so a password is required to log in.

- Remember, the internet is public. Even with privacy settings, "There is still a risk that private information could be exposed despite these restrictions, so don't post anything that you wouldn't want the public to see."[44] Sites occasionally change their privacy options, so make sure you regularly review your security and privacy settings.

- Be cautious of applications. Third-party applications often provide increased or new functionality or entertainment, but they often gain access to much of your information; some have malicious intent.

- As mentioned in Chapters 1 and 7, keep a good anti-malware solution updated on your device.

CHAPTER 9

Secure in Your Local Network

To start, let's be clear: this chapter does not explain in detail *how* to secure your network. Part of the reason is, each networking environment is unique. With hundreds of different network components available, attempting to explain each one would be futile. If you're looking for specifics, you can search the internet for your specific network components and how to configure them. Or, you can find someone to help you out.

As we move through this chapter, keep in mind the "local network" or "network" will normally refer to the immediate environment of your home or work. Typical networks connect to a gateway and from there go out to the internet, which is any website or location outside of the local network.

Wired, or Ethernet

I personally prefer connecting to an Ethernet port instead of wireless because the network signal is more reliable and less susceptible to interference. Of the network options, the Ethernet is the most secure because it requires a device to physically connect to the network. However, I usually connect to the wireless network at home because of convenience—I don't have many Ethernet ports at home.

Wireless

Wireless networks are the most common in homes and even most businesses. They are easy to set up and make it quick and convenient for people to access the network and internet. There are two general frequency bands used in Wi-Fi, the 2.4 and 5 gigahertz (GHz) frequencies. Most new routers can broadcast wireless internet on both 2.4 and 5 GHz bands.

However, certain frequencies of wireless networking, specifically the 2.4 GHz band, are more susceptible to interference from other devices. I've had issues with microwaves, baby monitors, and old cordless phones. Usually the issues have been with older devices using the network. Many older devices will only be able to use the 2.4 GHz frequency.

The advantage of the 2.4 GHz frequency is it usually has a longer range than the 5 GHz band and can often go through walls better.

The 5 GHz frequency can offer much faster speeds. However, if you don't need a faster network connection, then the 2.4 GHz should be sufficient—you won't see much of a difference in checking your email, but you might if you're streaming videos.

With both frequencies, the more devices connected to the same frequency, the slower the network speed will be. If you have a lot of devices, consider connecting devices that don't need faster speeds to the 2.4 GHz band and connecting the remaining devices to the 5 GHz.

Security-wise, Wi-Fi signals can be detected by a device with an appropriate network adapter. A network traffic analyzer, also known as a sniffer, can be used to capture all the network communication. On secure networks, this captured data is unintelligible. The danger is on open networks, those that don't require a password to access. Because these open (and usually free) networks are not encrypted, anyone using a sniffer on the Wi-Fi will be able to see and read the unencrypted network communications. This is why you should not use open Wi-Fi without using a VPN to securely access the internet. This is also the reason you should not provide open Wi-Fi on your home or business network.

Router/access points

Where your router is concerned, one of the first things you need to do is log in to its administration site. Because there are hundreds of routers, there is no way for me to provide exact instructions on how to log in or make changes. Your best option is an internet search on the brand and model of your router for a user manual or a how-to video.

Here are the basic steps for setting up a router:

First you need to connect to the router. After it's powered up, the best option is to use an Ethernet cable to directly connect to one of the local area network ports on the router. Many home routers with Wi-Fi have a few of these LAN ports. With some newer routers, you can connect to the administration site wirelessly, but I've found the most reliable connection to be through a LAN port.

Second, you need to go to the router's administration page by typing the IP address into a web browser. The user guide or instruction manual will identify what address to go to. Most of these IP addresses either start with "192.168" or "10.0," which are private IP address ranges, meaning they are not accessible to someone from outside of your private network. The instructions should give you the default username and password to log in to the administration site.

Once you are logged in to the page, you can configure various settings. Some of these are the name of the wireless network, wireless security, and various other controls such as allowing/disallowing certain devices and limiting network access times.

On some routers you can even set up a separate network, like a guest or kids' network, to which you can apply specific settings.

The most important thing to change in the router's administration site is the default name and password for the administrator account.

Security

Remember the discussion earlier about networking and the difference between public and private IP addresses?

At a very basic level, private IP addresses do provide a certain amount of protection to devices. Many attacks are directed to public IP addresses. If an attack happens to hit the router of the local area network, the router is basically dropped because there is no information as to where the attack should be directed within the private IP addresses.

However, if you've clicked on a bad link or gone to a malicious website, your device has already established a connection.

If the attacker can reach your router, they may be able to access its administration site. If you haven't changed the default password, it's only a matter of determining what kind of router you have and looking up the default administrator login credentials. This is why you need to change the default administrator username and, more importantly, the password.

You may want to create a guest network, or a specific network for children, if the router has that capability. By doing so, you can assign a different access password for that network and not have to give out the password to your main network.

The separate network may also have its own settings. For example, if the network is for children, you may want to limit internet access from 9 a.m. to 9 p.m. so the kids aren't online too late. You can use the excuse of the network cutting them off, instead of directly being the bad guy by making them get off.

When you configure the wireless network, you need to decide what kind of security it will have. The security is setting an encryption on the wireless communication. There are basically two parts to this security: the key (or password) and the type of wireless encryption.

For your password, choose one that is strong. The type of security encryption you choose determines how secure your network is. Some of the encryptions are much less secure and can be easily cracked.

WEP

WEP, or wired equivalent privacy, encryption is the oldest and least secure. Using freely available tools, almost anyone can easily learn to hack WEP. If you're using this encryption on your network, stop using it. Upgrade your wireless router if it doesn't offer anything more secure. If you have legacy devices that can only use WEP, you should upgrade the device or have a separate network connection for that device.

WPA

Wi-Fi Protected Access (WPA) came after WEP. WPA was developed to give extra protection for network security, but this was only a step towards the security standards of WPA2.

WPA incorporated a new security standard called Temporal Key Integrity Protocol (sounds like something out of sci-fi), or TKIP, which had several enhancements over WEP. The only reason to continue using TKIP is if a device can only connect over an 802.11g connection (more on this later).

WPA2

Most routers and Wi-Fi encryption should be using WPA2. With this version, the security protocol was based on Advanced Encryption Standard (AES), which is the U.S. Government's preferred encryption.

WPS

In 2007, Wi-Fi Protected Setup (WPS) was introduced. It allows users to connect a device to the network by simply pushing a button on the device, or through some administration software, and then entering an

8-digit PIN on the device. The premise was that having physical access to the wireless access point to push a button, and add a device, would be a more secure Wi-Fi authentication method.

But, a security flaw was recently discovered. The eighth digit of the PIN is actually a checksum number, which makes sure the other seven aren't corrupted. Then, instead of checking the seven remaining digits as a single number, which would have 10,000,000 possibilities, the number is split into two: a four-digit number (10,000 possibilities) and a three-digit number (1,000) possibilities. So, there are actually only 11,000 possible codes, which can be cracked with a few hours.[54]

So, while convenient, for security purposes, don't use WPS.

WPA3

This latest version of WPA promises better security, including

- increased protection from brute force attacks, where attackers try to break in using every possible password they can;
- encryption that is individualized between the device and router;
- increased security for Internet of Things (see Chapter 10); and
- stronger encryption levels, which will substantially increase wireless security.

For our general discussion of Wi-Fi security, here's the summary:

- Don't use WEP. It's the weakest and easiest to crack.
- Don't use WPS, as it's also easily hacked into.
- WPA should only be used if a legacy device requires it.
- Use WPA2.
- When it's available, use WPA3 with a strong passphrase, as it'll be the more secure option.

When you get into the wireless security settings of the router, you may encounter different offerings of WPA2, such as Pre-Shared Key (PSK) mode and Enterprise mode. For most home Wi-Fi networks, and even many small businesses, the PSK mode will be used. Basically, this mode requires you to set up the Wi-Fi password on the router, and users wanting to use the Wi-Fi need to use that password.

The WPA2-Enterprise mode involves much more configuration and utilization of an authentication server. This mode is government-grade wireless security and has several enhancements. For most home and small business networks, this is probably bordering overkill.

Regardless of how you want to set up the wireless security on the network, if you have questions, refer to the user manual, look up the support site of the router's manufacturer, read how-to articles, or even watch videos. If one article or video doesn't make sense, check another. My experience is there are a lot of poorly made videos/articles, so if you encounter a bad one, don't waste your time finishing it. A few gems do an excellent job in presenting the material.

802 Standards

Most likely you have seen numbers with 802, such as 802.11, usually with "a," "b," "g," "n," or combinations like "an" or "ax" after the numbers.

The number "802" refers to a group of network standards established by the Institute of Electrical and Electronic Engineers (IEEE). The 802.3 standards are for Ethernet, your wired network, and the 802.11 standards govern wireless networking, which is why your wireless router has one or more of the 802.11 letters associated with it.

Also, among those standards are the 802.1x standard for applying authentication and the 802.11i standard, applying to security on wireless networks; WPA protocols implement most of these standards.

The main takeaway is there are networking and security standards that manufacturers generally comply with.

It may be of interest that the Wi-Fi Alliance is wanting to simplify the names of the various networking technologies, renaming them to Wi-Fi 4, Wi-Fi 5, and Wi-Fi 6. The specifications will still follow the IEEE standards; the idea is just to make it simpler for people to understand.

CHAPTER 10

Internet of Things

It seems like you can buy just about anything that can connect to the internet, or at least to your home network. A common term for this connectivity is "smart." The general increase in connectivity of devices to each other and the internet is known as the Internet of Things (IoT).

By 2020, the number of IoT devices and sensors, just in the consumer market, is predicted to be almost 13 billion. This growth means more devices are vulnerable to attacks, and your security and privacy are threatened from more sides. "In 2018, there was a 5,400 percent increase in the number of IoT vulnerabilities recorded over the number reported just five years earlier."[55]

Smart devices

All it takes is a stroll in a home improvement store or furniture/appliance retailer, and you will discover almost every major appliance has a "smart" option.

Smart TVs have been around for a while, although they are getting smarter. But smart refrigerators and other appliances are relatively new. Add to that smart light bulbs, thermostats, sprinkler systems, home security systems, small appliances, and a wide array of other devices. All are meant to make your life easier, more convenient, and more efficient.

Making regular household devices smart

With all the new smart devices, what about the older, non-smart ones? For many of them, you can add an element of connectivity and control.

For example, you can buy smart switches and outlets. These don't make the old devices "smart," but they do add some controllability to them.

In our home, I've bought four smart outlets. They're more like outlet extensions you plug into the outlet and then plug your device into them. They're primarily used to control and set timers for lights. When we're away, I can log in to my smartphone and either manually turn lights on or off or activate some rules I've set to automatically control the lights.

The hazards of IoT

One of the hazards of IoT is the lack of standards between different brands and even differing devices. While this can make it more challenging for an attacker, it also leaves little incentive for manufacturers to make their devices more secure.

Because of the limited functionality of the operating systems on IoT devices, these systems don't have anti-malware applications, and identifying malware-infected devices can be difficult.

Many internet-connected devices can end up exposing your home network through that connection. Some of the devices have very little security on them. Often the default settings are left unchanged, which means anyone, from anywhere, can log in to the device, if they can access the device from the internet.

Leaving the default setting unchanged may also make your device useful in an attack. In 2016, the Mirai botnet was actually comprised mostly of IoT devices that had been compromised through various flaws and security vulnerabilities. The botnet caused worldwide internet disruption and was a wake-up call to the vulnerabilities of IoT devices. Other botnets have since taken advantage of similar vulnerabilities. Besides DDoS attacks, malware on IoT devices are used in cryptomining and brute force attacks, where an attacker tries to break into a system using lists of usernames and passwords.

Unfortunately, as manufacturers rush to produce new and better products, security is usually an afterthought, so more devices will have vulnerabilities.[56] Raytheon, who sponsored a Ponemon Institute 2018 Study on Global Megatrends in Cybersecurity, discovered the following about IoT security:

- According to 82 percent of the respondents, unsecured IoT devices will likely be the cause of a data breach in their organization, and 80 percent said the breach would be catastrophic.
- These professionals also said IoT devices are among the technologies that "will pose the greatest cyber risk over the next three years."[57]

If the risks are increasing for businesses and other organizations, you can be certain IoT risks are increasing in homes.

Securing TVs, network cameras, and other IoT devices

The first thing to do on any network-connected device is to change the default administrator password. If the device doesn't have a password, it shouldn't be connected to the internet. Using botnets and programs to scan the web, cybercriminals will find devices using default administrator credentials and exploit them.

The other step in securing a smart device is regularly updating its software and/or firmware. Some devices may have automatic updates. Most will likely require you to log in to the system and manually check for updates or to set up the automatic updates.

CHAPTER 11

Secure in the World-*Wild* Web

Sometimes the internet, also known as the worldwide web, is compared to the wild west. The openness of the web has significantly increased communication and sharing of information. But, there is a wild part that we need to be wary of.

We typically access the internet through a web browser. Over the years new features and standards have been developed for browsers and websites to increase our security. There are too many different browsers and versions of those browsers to get into specifics. However, there are some general security items you should be aware of that are applicable across browsers.

Secure websites

Secure sites are becoming more of the norm than they used to be. You can identify a secure site by the "https" at the beginning of the web address. Some browsers may display a lock icon (sometimes it's green) before the web address. In any case, whenever possible, look for a secure website. This is especially true if you are asked to log in to a site.

The "s" at the end of "https" refers to "secure." This indicates the site uses a security certificate, which is verified by a third-party certificate authority. Web traffic between your browser and the site is encrypted, so your communication is kept secure.

While a secure site is not a guarantee it's a safe site, it's a big step in that direction. Most malicious sites are not secure and don't have the "https" as part of the web address. I have encountered the rare malicious site that seems to employ a security certificate, but it's not common and the security certificate may be a compromised one.

In any case, more legitimate sites are using security certificates, even on pages that don't require a login.

Browser security

Like anything that has software code, keep your browser up-to-date. Most browsers are set to automatically update, so usually all you need to do is close and relaunch the browser when an update is ready to be installed. In most browsers you can check for updates in the Help or About section, or the look for Check for Updates in the browser settings.

Unless you need to change settings, most browsers have a decent security setting to begin with. There are tweaks you can make for increased security as well other tweaks that make it less secure.

These are just some of the many settings you can adjust in a browser:

- Set your home page and default search engines.
- Allow or block sites—block bothersome sites or allow one that may not normally be permitted.
- Adjust pop-up permissions, from prohibiting them to permitting their use on some sites, where pop-ups are required for site functionality.
- Block content based on certain criteria.
- View, add, enable, disable, or remove browser add-ons, plug-ins, or extensions.
- Set the automatic browser updates, and manually check for updates.
- Clear data stored by the browser, such as sites visited (history), form data, and other information.

There are many other features and functionality you can configure in the browser.

Be aware that there are many malicious add-ons, plug-ins, and extensions for browsers. Often these are installed unintentionally. Some of the malicious changes to the browser include modifying home pages and default search engines or adding new toolbars or other browser extensions.

Cookies

Unfortunately, these aren't the ones you eat. You've probably heard references to cookies on the computer or browser, or maybe someone told you to clear the cookies. If you don't know what these are, you're not the first.

Cookies are very small text files that are stored on your computer when you visit websites. They store some data, like your preferences, but most are harmless. There are different types of cookies.

Session cookies track you when you log on to a site. They store information related to your login, referred to as a session ID, but not your username and password. After you log in and are authenticated to access the site, the browser is given a session cookie so you can go from one site page to the next, without having to log in to each page separately. If the session cookie didn't exist, you'd be logging in to almost every page. When you log out or close the browser, the session cookie is supposed to be deleted and is no longer valid.

Site cookies are usually more general. They may store personal preferences, search information, and some computer-related information. Site cookies are readable by the web server that placed them, which makes it easier and more convenient for you when you return to the site, by better customizing your visit.

There are also advertising-related cookies. If you've ever gone to a site, searched for something you were interested in buying, decided not to, went to another site, and then saw ads for the item you previously searched for, then you experienced the effect of an advertising cookie. The cookie has a unique user ID from the advertiser (the company you previously visited). When you visit another site, if that site uses an online ad company to serve ads, the ad company uses the user ID to help identify what ads might be more relevant to you.

Cookies are mostly used to help you receive a more customized experience on the web. If you want, you can go into the browser's settings to adjust preferences for cookies. Because cookies may store some data that some consider private, many sites have requested your permission for the site to use cookies. If you choose not to accept the cookies, then your experience with the site probably won't be optimized.

Generally, cookies are not a security risk. However, some sites and search engines use cookies to track users and collect very personal information about them. These less reputable sites may even transfer your information to other websites without your permission or warning.

If you happen on one of these less-than-ethical sites, you might start getting browser-based adware, or your homepage and/or default search engine may have changed. You may notice a new toolbar. Clearing the data stored by the browser, including the cookies, as well as correcting any changes made often gets things back to normal. Sometimes resetting the browser becomes necessary.

Some anti-malware may not identify these browser-based issues. Other anti-malware may identify these as "potentially unwanted programs," but they won't be quarantined or deleted unless you request it.

Some sites will ask if you want to have your device remembered or registered. Registering your device will usually set a site cookie on your device so your next login is easier. If the site doesn't recognize your device, you may be asked additional security questions or have other security measures to go through. Registering your device usually bypasses these additional questions. Personally, I'd rather answer the extra questions. If my device is used by someone else, the site wouldn't know it's not me, so I'd rather keep the security higher.

There are a few theories about where the term "cookie" comes from. Personally, I think the most likely candidate is the story of Hansel and Gretel. Although most accounts of the story have the children leaving bread crumbs, cookie crumbs would do the job. Someone probably decided "cookie" sounded better than "bread" for a tracking file.

Remembering passwords & other info

I'm not a fan of a browser remembering my password. This feature is for convenience and ease of use. But, if the browser remembers it, it's just another point where my information can be compromised. Besides, if someone else gets on the browser, they'll have direct access into the site's account.

My password manager allows me to drag-and-drop my usernames and passwords into login fields, so it's almost as convenient as the browser remembering my information, but it's a lot more secure.

As for the browser remembering other information, like addresses and other items used to auto-fill forms, that's up to you. Again, if the browser remembers this information, it means another place where some personal information could be compromised. What information is stored is found in the browser's settings.

In the browser's settings, you can clear any saved information as well as cookies, history, and other data stored by the browser. You can also reset the browser to erase stored information.

Log out

When you are done on a site, make sure you log out. This should release the session cookie and let the site (and browser) know you're done. Most of the time, closing the browser will also terminate the session.

If you don't log out and you're on a public computer—or a device that others might access should you step away—someone could get onto the site with your account. For this reason, most sites use a session inactivity time-out, where you are automatically logged out of your account after a specified time of inactivity.

Internet service provider content filtering

In 2018, the Utah legislature passed a bill modifying Utah code with regards to the responsibility of an internet service provider (ISP) to offer content filtering methods for material harmful to minors. The service provider is to notify all of its Utah residential customers of the option to request harmful material be blocked.

Other states may also have content filtering laws to help protect minors.

Some ISPs provide apps and settings to help parents or guardians manage internet access for children. Some of the features that may be available include

- viewing internet activity,
- managing apps on mobile devices,
- finding teacher-recommended apps,
- setting time limits,
- remotely locking a device, and
- locating the child (if the mobile device is with them).

Before you buy online

Use only secure payment options, such as credit cards or PayPal. Whenever possible, avoid using debit, checking, or savings account information for online payments. Payments tied to checking or savings accounts put your money at greater risk first and are harder to get corrected in the case of fraud. Using credit cards, or similar payment options, put a buffer between the payment and your money. If there's fraud or incorrect charges, you can dispute the charges before they are paid. Payments from checking or savings accounts are taken straight from the account, and you're out that amount for however long it takes to resolve the dispute.

It's best to avoid sites that require you to use a wire transfer, money order, or other unsecured (and nonrefundable) forms of payment.

If the deal's too good to be true, it probably is. Walk/click away from it. There are sites offering deep discounts, but these are usually on older goods and models.

Research the seller before you buy. A quick online search can reveal a lot. Are there reviews? If not, that could be a concern. Are there a lot of negative reviews? Better keep away. You can also look up companies through the Better Business Bureau's website, at www.bbb.org.

Account recovery

If you can't log in to an account—if your username and password are not recognized and can't be reset—you may need to recover the account. Account recovery might be needed if

- your account information, like your password, was changed by someone;
- your account was deleted by someone; or
- you're unable to sign in to your account.

Many sites offer account recovery options. On older sites, these options were often added later, and you need to log in to the site and set up the recovery options. On newer sites, and those which have undergone improvements, I've found at least a few recovery options are required. These might be a secondary email, smartphone, or some other way to authenticate a recovery request. In the interest of the security and privacy of your information, make sure you set up account recovery options.

CHAPTER 12

Phone and Mobile Security

I wasn't old enough to have the brick cell phone, but my first cell phone wasn't small. It didn't have text messaging. Now smartphones are small computers, and it's projected mobile phone users will exceed 5 billion in 2019.[58]

There has been an extensive push towards securing computers, networks, and systems, but mobile security has been lagging. The rapid evolution of smart devices has outpaced security efforts, making them more vulnerable targets.

For many people, their mobile phone might contain more sensitive data than their computer. If the device is connected to a corporate network, it may contain sensitive work-related data as well. What's more, the smartphone is more likely to get lost or stolen.

For attackers, mobile devices are increasingly becoming an attractive attack point. One example is phishing. On the computer, the attacker can basically attack only through email. But, the phone allows the hacker to phish through emails, texts, and even calls. Infected and malicious apps—posing to be legitimate ones—can be installed and can then download malware to the device.

Downloading apps through the official mobile stores (such as Apple Store and Google Play Store) are the best option, as they have security controls. However, some malware and infected apps still manage to get into the store.

Here is an interesting study to consider. Back in 2011, IBM accessed the log files of several web servers conducting phishing attacks. The first few hours of a phishing attack are the most critical for the hacker because after that, phishing filters have been adjusted and the attacks are blocked or the websites are discovered and taken down. Here's what the study discovered:

- Mobile users are the first to fall into the snare.
- Mobile users are three times more likely to submit personal information, including account credentials, than desktop computer users.[59]

It was surmised the reason behind these observations are that mobile users are "always on" and most likely to read, and respond to, emails as soon as the message arrives. Since these fraudulent emails are often urgent sounding and call for immediate action, the mobile users are more likely to do so.

Additionally, identifying a fraudulent email on a mobile device can be more difficult. One reason may be that the "from" address often displays the sender's name but not the email address. This may lead some users into thinking the device trusts the sender. When users can see the entire "from" address and it looks "phishy," they're less likely to open the message.

Viewing email on a mobile device can also make it hard to identify where a link will actually go when it is clicked/touched. When the site comes up on the browser, the actual address is often hidden, as the small display adjusts to maximize site viewing. Since most phishing sites are good clones of real sites, it's not easy to identify a fake site on a mobile device.

Another security issue to be aware of when using mobile devices relates to password security. Some users store their passwords on the phone, such as in a Contacts listing or in a notes file. In any case, it's not a good idea to put your passwords where someone could read them. Use a password manager. From the manager, you should be able to drag-and-drop or copy-and-paste your credentials to the sites you need to access, or you can view the information to log in on another device.

Protecting your phone number

Because your cell phone is increasingly important, you need to protect it in case it's lost or stolen. Encrypting the information and setting a password, or other login, helps keep your data protected. But, you also need to protect your phone number.

Hackers could get the cell number of their target, call the cell phone carrier, and impersonate their target, especially if the hacker has some basic information. Often the information is little more than an address and birthdate. The hacker might ask to "port" (transfer) the number to another carrier or a different SIM card. As soon as the number is active on the new phone, the hacker can make and receive calls and messages. As for victims, the only clue they have is their phone loses cell service.

From there, the hacker might be able to use the phone to reset passwords, steal data, and access accounts.

Your main defense is to set up a secondary security code on your phone account, such as a PIN or passcode. You can do this by calling your cell carrier; some even allow this to be done online. Make sure the code is applied to all account changes and all numbers on the account. Anyone calling to make changes on the phone account would have to give that PIN or passcode. Try to have a code that's longer than the normal four to six digits, and keep a backup of that code in a safe place.

Securing your mobile device

If a lot of these recommendations seem familiar, they are.

- Regularly back up the data on your device.

- Keep your device's OS updated. Just like in other computing systems, OS patches and updates are frequently issued and need to be applied.
- Regularly update the apps. These may get updated automatically, but some updates may require your approval. You should regularly check to see if updates are available.
- Don't trust unsecured, public Wi-Fi networks, and use a VPN when you do connect to public Wi-Fi.
- Enable the PIN, password lock, or other security on your device. You don't want someone to instantly access your device (and the data on it) should it be left unattended.
- Use encryption for securing sensitive information stored on your device.
- Look at the permissions an app is requesting before you install it. Don't install apps that ask for too much information, especially if there isn't a good reason for it.
- Install anti-malware or security software only from a valid source. There are lots of malware posing as security applications.
- Don't download apps from unofficial websites. If you need to, be extra careful and have anti-malware protection installed.
- Enable the "Find My iPhone" (Apple) or "Find my Android" (Google) settings on your device so you can find a lost device and lock the phone or erase the data if it's stolen.
- Never open unexpected and unverified documents, even from a known source. If you're unsure, call and verify it's a legitimate document.
- Enable two-factor authentication for your accounts.
- Be wary of emails asking for personal information, especially usernames and passwords.
- Set the automatic screen lock on the device.

Several of these tips are related to phishing-style attacks. From my experience, it can be more difficult to determine valid emails on the smartphone than on a computer. Let's look at an example.

The following screenshot is from the email app on my phone. Supposedly the email is from the Apple store.

Figure 19: A mobile view of a phishing email.

It's difficult to tell if the email is legitimate or phishy, so more information is needed. On the email I pressed the "Details" to see more information.

Figure 20: Another mobile view of the same phishing email. The "Details" option was clicked, which only revealed the "To" address.

The additional details weren't very helpful. The only real clue is the "To" address shows an email address @appstore.com.au. This wouldn't be much except, why isn't the "To" address to me? And, why would I be getting something from the Australian Apple store site and not the regular .com site?

Let's look at the same email, but from the Microsoft Outlook email client.

Mon 1/21/2019 4:15 AM

Apple Payment <rencananyamauspamsapaipagitadi927·64804863@investingchicken.com>
receipt from Apple store.

To cs@appstore.com.au

Archive 7/20/2019

You forwarded this message on 1/21/2019 8:28 AM.

Message E-receiptMacBook3731638.pdf (263 KB)

Dear Apple customers,

Your account is limited due to suspicious activity. Please cancel your purchase within 48 hours, open the file (PDF)

Greetings,

Apple.

Figure 21: The same phishing email (as Figures 9 and 10) viewed from Microsoft's Outlook email client on a PC. Note the "From" email.

Beside a bigger viewing screen, we can see a big red flag in this view. The email "From" address is some address from the site @investingchicken.com.

You may also note that I forwarded the message. What it doesn't show is that I forwarded it to the institutions spam reporting service so it could be added to the spam filters.

Methods of authentication

There are several ways you can log in to (authenticate) your phone or mobile device. New methods, including combinations, are continuously being developed and improved. We'll look briefly at several and mention some of the advantages and disadvantages for each. Some of these may also be authentication methods for other computing devices.

Password (passphrase)

As previously discussed, a long, strong passphrase is very secure. However, strong passwords can be difficult to type using the small virtual keyboards of a mobile device. This difficulty increases when you need to switch between different keyboards to get numbers, letters, and special characters. Strong passwords are also inconvenient to type in if you have to do it multiple times in a short period.

PIN

A personal identification number (PIN) is much easier to enter than a passphrase, but most PINs are too short to be secure. Secure PINs have the disadvantage of being difficult to remember.

Pattern lock

A lot of people like the pattern lock option because it's considered simple and intuitive. The interface involves using your finger to draw a pattern among nine dots on the screen. The pattern can usually be any number of dots, from four to all nine. The finger movement can be vertical, horizontal, and/or diagonal. Because swiping can feel more natural than entering a PIN, unlocking the phone with a pattern can be quicker and easier.

However, the number of dots you choose to use will determine the strength of the pattern. A four-dot pattern has only 1,624 combinations. If you use eight or nine dots in a pattern, there are 140,701 possible combinations.[60]

Unfortunately, most people use only four or five dots. Seventy-seven percent of users start their pattern in one of the corners, and over 10 percent make their pattern in the shape of a letter, most likely the first initial of their name or someone close to them.[61] Using these common practices, the number of likely patterns drops to a few hundred.

If you use a pattern lock, follow these recommendations:

- Don't start the pattern in a corner.
- Don't use the shape of a letter.
- Use as many dots as possible.
- Turn off the "make pattern visible" option, making it harder for someone to shoulder-surf and see you pattern.

Fingerprint

Fingerprint authentication can be fast and secure. But, the sensors aren't always in a convenient spot. If you wear gloves, you need to take them off or use another method to unlock your phone. Another issue is that some fingerprint sensors are more responsive than others. A cut or bandaged finger can cause difficulties with some sensors. My experience with fingerprint scanners is they can use improvement.

Be aware that when it comes to certain biometrics, there is disagreement in the courts as to whether someone can be forced to unlock a device with their fingerprint, face, or other biometric factor. Prior to 2019 the courts had ruled using a fingerprint, or other biometric input, wasn't a fifth amendment issue, although passwords could not be forcibly divulged. However, in early 2019, a California judge ruled that law enforcement cannot force people to unlock a device using their face or finger. Most likely this ruling will be appealed and ruled on at a district court (or higher) level.

Facial recognition

Perhaps one of the most convenient methods of unlocking your phone is through facial recognition. How the recognition is implemented on the device will partly determine its security. If the method uses 2D imaging, the system can be more easily fooled. The 3D imaging is a little more secure. However, facial recognition is still a work in progress. Certain systems can struggle to identify users in different lighting or if glasses are worn.

Iris scanner

Iris scanners are one of the more secure forms of biometric identification, although lighting conditions (particularly bright light), glasses, or contacts may cause some difficulties. The iris scanner scans both eyes and requires a little more work than facial recognition, as it usually requires you to hold down a button and position the device in the right place to scan your eyes.

Combination

There are also sign-ins that combine a few methods, such as a facial and iris scan.

Other options to unlock the device

Some devices provide other options to unlock your phone within certain parameters. For Android-based phones, some of those options are on-body detection, trusted places, trusted devices, trusted face, and voice match.

On-body detection unlocks the phone when it senses you carrying it. But it could just as well unlock if someone else is carrying it.

With trusted places, the phone unlocks itself when it's in a specific location, such as home or office. And, it'll still unlock if an unauthorized user has it in the trusted place.

The trusted device option unlocks the phone when it's within range of a specified Bluetooth device. The range is typically up to 30 feet.

Trusted face unlocks the device when the camera detects an authorized face. This feature may be combined with facial recognition.

Voice match unlocks your phone when a key phrase is used, such as "OK Google." This feature is useful in a hands-free situation.

Remember, these options are for your convenience, making your device easier to use. However, convenience has a way of making it easier for the bad guys also.

Spam/spoofed calls

Most of us with cell phones have been receiving robocalls from numbers that are similar to our own, with the same area code and often a similar prefix. Known as neighbor spoofing, or NPA-NXX spoofing (NPA is the area code, and NXX is the local exchange in technical jargon), it's a form of caller ID spoofing, where the spammer uses technology to make the phone number displayed on your phone appear to be from your local area. The intent is to increase the odds you'll pick up the phone. Many of us do end up answering the call because we think it might be an important call, like from a school or doctor or from a client if we use our phone for work.

The Federal Communications Commission (FCC) is trying to work with the phone industry to create and adopt the use of a caller ID authentication system. The intent of this system is to fight against illegal caller ID spoofing and to help ensure legitimate calls are permitted. In November 2018, the FCC chairman, Ajit Pai, "demanded that the phone industry adopt a robust call authentication system to combat illegal caller ID spoofing and launch that system no later than next year."[62] We will see whether the carriers will implement the system on their own or if regulatory intervention will happen.

Dealing with spoofed calls

Here are a few tips that may help avoid neighbor spoofing robocalls:

- Register your phone number with the National Do Not Call Registry: https://www.donotcall.gov/. This won't stop callers from illegal operations, but it may stop some calls from legitimate telemarketers.
- Don't answer calls from numbers you don't recognize. Let the call go to voicemail. If the call's important, the caller will usually leave a voicemail.

- If you do answer what turns out to be a robocall, hang up immediately.
- If the caller, or recording, asks you to press a button to stop getting calls, don't do it. Just hang up. Pressing the number lets the scammer know your phone number is valid, and they'll use it to identify potential targets.
- Don't respond to any questions, particularly with "yes" or "no" answers.

Personally, I will almost never return a call to an unknown number if no voicemail was left. I have answered the occasional call from someone trying to return a missed call (a call supposedly from my phone number). Most of the time the caller understands when I explain I didn't make the call, and it's just an unfortunate waste of time, on both sides.

Because I do use my phone for work, there are occasionally calls from numbers I don't recognize. For me in this case, it's not always the best option to let the caller go to voicemail, so answering is a risk I sometimes take to provide customer service.

I also know there are times when potential clients may be calling, and they may not want to leave a message. If you don't answer the call, you may risk losing business.

In cases where it makes business sense, or you just get too many robocalls, you may look into whether your cell carrier provides a solution to stop spam calls, although these services often incur an additional monthly fee. There are also applications to reduce robocalls and neighbor spoofing.

Here are a few additional tips for dealing with spam callers:

- Never give out any personal information or confirm any information, such as account numbers, Social Security numbers, your mother's maiden name, passwords, etc. in response to any unexpected or suspicious calls.

- If the caller claims to be a representative from a company or a government agency, hang up and call the number on your account statement or on the company or government agency website and verify the request. Remember, if the caller is asking for payment, you will usually have gotten a written statement regarding the payment before you get a call from a legitimate source.

- Be cautious if you're being pressured to provide immediate information or payment; these are red flags for scams.

- Set a voicemail account password. Some voicemail is set to allow immediate access to the account if you call from your phone number. If a hacker gets your number, they could spoof it and access your voicemail, if the account doesn't have a password set.

If you get calls about your number showing up on a caller ID and you didn't make the call, politely explain you didn't make the call. Most of the time scammers will change numbers frequently, so it's likely within a few hours they'll be using a different number.

The Truth in Caller ID Act prohibits misleading or inaccurate caller ID information, specifically with the intent to defraud, cause harm, or wrongly obtain anything of value. Illegal spoofing can lead to fines of $10,000 per violation. But, the reality is, most scammers are operating from outside the country.

There are legitimate uses for spoofing. Some of these instances are when a doctor calls from a personal mobile device, and the number of the doctor's office is displayed instead. Or, a call from a business might display the toll-free call-back number. Hopefully by the end of 2019 we'll see some positive changes towards reducing illegal robocalls.

CHAPTER 13

Protecting Your Family Online

Protecting your family digitally is a challenging and ever-changing conundrum for parents. Technology evolves quickly. New applications appear, and many take a shooting star to a brief, bright popularity before being snuffed out and replaced by the next big thing.

By no means is this brief chapter going to cover, or even attempt to cover, everything that can be done to help protect families on the world *wild* web. Additionally, I am not an expert in child development or in marriage and family counseling.

However, my wife and I have four children, and I'm getting some real-world experience with raising children, unlike some experts who may not even have a child. My first bachelor's degree was in recreation management and youth leadership, and I've spent more than eight seasons working with teenagers. So, while I'm not a certificated or licensed expert, I have some understanding of what is involved and the inherent challenges. From my personal experience and observations, here are some of ideas for you to consider.

Children and the web

Children are naturally curious. It also seems that children are quick to pick up the use of technology.

The problem is, while children quickly adapt to technology, they are often unaware of security and privacy implications of their online actions, which could expose not only their personal information but yours as well. Unless they're educated otherwise, this doesn't change as they grow up, especially when it comes to giving away information through social media.

When I was growing up, the joke (which was too often true) was the parents or grandparents asked the child to program the VCR so it'd stop blinking "12:00."

The tech has evolved, but the scenario isn't much different. My kids quickly learn to use their fingers to navigate touchscreens. I've seen, and heard of, instances where a child changes some setting on a device and the parent, or grandparent, is completely baffled on how it happened—and even more stumped trying to return the device back to normal.

One of the worst things a parent can do is absolutely forbid and ban children from using technology. When those children are free from the parent's oversight, they may be more likely to binge on technology and more willingly go online unsupervised.

The other extreme—to give the child free, unlimited, uncontrolled, and unsupervised access to technology—is just as bad. Many parents relent to a child's demands for whatever tech is in demand: a new gaming system, new smartphone, etc. The child uses the old tune, just modernized, that "everyone else has the XYZ device" and they'll be left out. Too often when the parent gives the child the XYZ device, the parent does it without knowing much about what the XYZ does or can do and without any type of parental control or supervision.

Introducing a child to the internet should be done incrementally. Though it would be time consuming to allow them access to each site individually, a smart idea is to let them prove to you they are responsible and trustworthy. Teaching them to navigate safely through the web is ultimately the responsibility of the parent or guardian.

When should a child get a smartphone?

The real answer is, it depends. Other than needing to call a parent or a few other select, trusted adults and family, a child does not "need" a smartphone. However, by about the fourth grade, it may be good for a child to have a phone to call you. Phone restrictions can be set to only call designated numbers. The phone should be locked down so they can't use it for other purposes, particularly on the web.

A lot of people have the fear of missing out (FOMO, as it's sometimes called). The phone buzzes, beeps, or blinks with some notification, and the recipient immediately, even subconsciously, reaches for the phone to check it. We are easily distracted by our phones. Kids, including teenagers, are no different. Unless the child has amazing self-control, or has been removed from the device, smartphones are a distraction in school.

A study from University of Nebraska-Lincoln found, on average, students spend "20 percent of their classroom time using digital devices for activities unrelated to class—mostly text messaging but also emailing, web-surfing, checking social media and even playing games."[45] Thirty percent believed they could still learn without being distracted from learning. About 13 percent said the benefit of using the devices outweighed the distractions, and 11 percent said they couldn't stop themselves. Eleven percent also reported spending more than 50 percent of class time on devices for non-class purposes.

While I think a phone (for calling) and, maybe, limited messaging may be needed when a child is young, they don't need unsupervised internet access until they can demonstrate responsible use. There are phone settings and apps that can be set up or installed, allowing a parent/guardian to control and monitor the smartphone use, including use of apps and internet access.

Two keys can help parents keep them be safe online. First, you need open and non-condemning communication with your child. Second, which is related to the first, your child needs to trust you and your unconditional love. Both of these need to start when the child is young.

If the child learns when they are young that you blow up, yell, condemn them, belittle them, or make them feel stupid, guilty, or fearful whenever they try to tell you something, particularly if it's something they are emotionally unsure about, then they probably won't come to you with questions about something they saw online. They'll go to their friends.

Your children need to feel you will listen and not condemn or belittle them for their mistakes. They need to feel safe in coming to you, and they need to trust you love them and want what is best for them.

Web security

You are responsible for teaching your children. If you don't, someone else will. Don't put off teaching your children about the hazards of the internet, including the danger of over-sharing. Many of their friends may have free access to computers, smartphones, and other mobile devices. Most have had no education concerning responsible use of those devices or the internet.

Parents and guardians must talk to their children about the internet, the good and the bad. Children need continual reminders, and teaching them about online predators is no different. These predators use social engineering and scams to lure children. They prey on children in gaming chat rooms, through social media, and in a wide variety of apps. Many predators are also sexual predators, who convince children and youth to send them explicit images and videos. When the child tries to back out, sexual extortion frequently follows, where the predator threatens to post the explicit videos and images unless the victim complies with demands. Children and youth have committed suicide because they're scared and don't know where to turn for help.

On mobile devices, access to the internet should be blocked or filtered with parental control, especially when you first give the child the device.

As they get older, and show they can be responsible and trustworthy, you can open up their access.

However, until the child has bought their own phone and pays for their own service, you have the right to access and restrict the phone you provide. You should never give them access to use your credit card (or other banking information) to buy an app, add-on, or other purchase. All new apps and purchases should go through you. When a new app is requested, you need to learn what the app is for by looking it up online; don't trust your child to tell you, because they probably don't really know much about the app—only that their friends are using it.

Some families use an internet service provider that provides filtered internet access, but there's no guarantee a questionable site won't be seen. Operators of pornographic sites know their offerings appear harmless but are ultimately as addictive as any drug. They cast their net wide to ensnare as many as might click on a link. But, for those operators, it's all about money. Many of these sites are infiltrated (either intentional or not) with links to malicious websites and applications. Not only are you being exposed to questionable material, but your device may be subject to malicious attacks as well.

Monitoring

Children need to know you have the option at any time to view the contents of whatever device they are using—and which you have provided and/or pay for. You should not become a tech tyrant, but you should occasionally view the apps and browsing history and ask questions. If you find something you're unfamiliar with, like some app, do an internet search on it, learn about it, and ask your child about it.

When you find something questionable, ask your child about it in a non-condemning way. Don't freak out. Don't overreact. Don't panic. Maybe you remember a mistake you made as a youth and how a parent or other adult may have reacted negatively when you revealed your mistake or asked a question that caught the adult off guard. Now you've discovered a mistake your child has made. Hopefully you and your child have open, trusting communication, which you can use to gently redirect your child toward better options.

Open computing

One way to help minimize questionable use of the computer in the family is to have it in a public place in the house. This doesn't mean where everybody is most of the time, where it may be difficult to use the computer for study. A "public place" in the house is a common room, where anybody can come in at any time, but it's not necessarily the home's grand central station.

Children, and especially youth, are less likely to go to questionable sites if they know anyone could walk in and see them. This doesn't imply that the child is intending to go to these sites. But, curiosity may override their sense, and, in a private room, they may be more likely to investigate.

Just as children should earn the privilege of increased smartphone capabilities, children should demonstrate their responsibility and trustworthiness before they get an internet-connected device in their room. I, personally, don't think this should happen until the youth is a junior or senior in high school.

Social media posting

Some young children tend to be overly trusting, and some freely share information that should be kept private. For example, a couple of my kids will freely tell our neighbors, or even someone walking down the street, when we're going out of town. They are still under age eight, so I'm hoping my wife and I can eventually convince them to not be so transparent about our family activities. Hopefully by the time they're old enough to have a social media account they'll be more responsible.

Regarding social media and children, I believe the age limit most social media sites impose (currently age 13 for a lot of them) is probably appropriate for some children. Technologically and socially active children will want to be more involved with social media, if for no other reason than because their friends are.

You need to teach your children the dangers of posting anything online. Always consider that anything posted online will likely stay online. Even those companies that promise to delete all your information upon request will have a difficult time tracking down all the places your photos and posts may have been copied or shared.

Some people believe that some apps will delete a post or image after a brief time and nobody will be able to see it after that. But, the supposedly deleted images on a device may be recoverable.

Back in 2013, a Utah-based company, Decipher Forensics, was able to recover images on an Android-based phone that were supposedly deleted by a popular photo-sharing application.[46] More recently, in 2017, a paper was published regarding research into forensic analysis of images and videos that were supposed to be deleted.[47]

Always treat everything you post as permanent. Privacy settings may help keep it contained, but don't count on those.

Child protection registry

The state of Utah has a free program called Utah Child Protection Agency that helps parents and guardians stop adult-oriented solicitations from targeting children and their family. The program allows for the protection of email addresses, mobile phone numbers, instant messenger IDs, and fax numbers. Any company sending out adult-oriented messages—such as those promoting pornography, alcohol, illegal drugs, tobacco, and gambling—must screen their lists with the state of Utah and remove registered addresses and numbers. Marketers failing to remove registered addresses face civil and criminal fines as well as felony charges.

While this registry is for residents of Utah, other states likely have similar laws and do-not-contact lists to protect minors.

Young children and development

If you have children in the home, it's important to realize your attitude and example towards computing devices are key in teaching a child how to value screen time. While the child may learn some safe practices, teaching privacy and security to your child is ultimately your responsibility.

I think it's also important to understand some of the hazards associated with screen time and children. While these hazards are not directly security oriented, they do apply to protecting children. Personally, I believe the more time children spend online can negatively affect their perception of online security. They become more comfortable and may be more likely to drop their guard.

Screen time

There is debate about how much screen time is good or bad. The American Academy of Pediatrics has previously set a general limit of two hours per day for screen time. They further recommended children 18 months and younger shouldn't have screen time, and those ages 2 to 5 shouldn't have more than 1 hour.[48] In 2018, one study's results suggested that limiting children's screen time to less than two hours per day was associated with improved cognition.[49]

In early 2019, the Royal College of Paediatrics and Child Health (RCPCH) published guidance for parents, stating, "There is not enough evidence to confirm that screen time is in itself harmful to child health at any age, making it impossible to recommend age appropriate time limits."[50] The guidance recommends parents base screen time on the child's developmental age and need, and to increase emphasis on exercise, sleep, and social activities. There is evidence that when screen time replaces these activities, there's an increased risk to the child's well-being. The real determinant is how much activity the child gets and not so much the amount of screen time.

Several studies have examined the effects of screen time on children and youth. One study, which is at the beginning of a decade-long period, is already showing significant early differences with those who spend more than seven hours a day on various screens. One result is a thinning of the cortex, the outermost layer of the brain. This usually doesn't happen until later in life. What this means isn't known.

There are reports of children entering school who are unable to hold pencils, pens, or even crayons because of having had too much technology.[51] The use of fingers to touch and swipe has resulted in a decline in the development of fine motor skills.[52]

The effects of technology aren't just in those entering school for the first time. A professor of surgical education at the Imperial College in London expressed concern that students have spent too much time in front of screens. Over the last decade, there has been a decline in the manual dexterity of students, where they have become "less competent and less confident"[53] with their hands, to the point that many struggle with simple stitches.

Personally, I think responsible technology use, and a big step towards better awareness of information security, begins with appropriate screen time limitations. As we become too involved in the virtual world, we can lose our awareness of what is safe. I believe our attitude towards security is affected by both our cybersecurity practices and physical security awareness.

I believe wise parents limit screen time appropriately and strongly encourage children to use their hands to color, draw, write, and play.

CHAPTER 14

Physical Security

Discussing physical security in a book about cybersecurity may seem a little out of place. The reality is, physical actions—such as card skimming, theft, or direct access to an unsecured device—lead to security incidents and data breaches.

The 2018 Verizon Data Breach Investigations Report (DBIR), which covers industries and not individuals, identified 3,930 incidents involving lost or stolen assets, and there were 145 confirmed data breaches from lost and stolen assets. If criminals can steal data from companies, they will certainly steal from individuals. That is why you need to be aware of and incorporate good physical security practices at work and home to secure personal information.

This chapter is not about securing all of your valuables, although many of the suggestions may help do that. And, while there may be some criminals who want to steal your personal documents, most are after the items they can sell quickly. We won't go into, or even mention, all the ways to increase physical security. Most might be considered common security recommendations, and many are applicable to home and business settings.

Instead, this chapter will focus on securing your personal information, which is stored on various devices in your home or business. Because electronics (including phones, tablets, computers, etc.) are targeted by thieves, you need to limit a thief's ability to steal them.

Physical security at work

Most workplaces, especially those with a lot of employees, use some kind of identification system. One of the more common is an ID badge.

Badges

In many cases, an ID badge is simply a card identifying someone. However, it's becoming more common for ID badges to have multiple functions. They may be used for clocking in and out. They may double as an access pass, allowing you to go into restricted areas protected by proximity locks.

Depending on the environment, ID badges may be required to be in full view, often worn on a lanyard or clipped to the clothing.

Verify authorization

If you work in a limited access environment, it's important to verify someone's identity. ID badges can be counterfeited, so if you don't recognize someone, ask some questions.

Hopefully your institution has access policies you can fall back on to use as an excuse to not help someone into a secure area. If someone claiming to have a delivery wants access through a secure entrance, you should direct them to the receiving area, or at least the front desk. Similarly, if an employee you don't know needs help getting in someplace requiring special access, it may seem unhelpful, but, it's best to have them go through the front desk or other place that will check their access qualifications. Use the policies as your excuse.

While this isn't directly related to security, it is related to verifying someone's identity. The place I work at holds a yearly training conference, and the department provides a lot of the audio-visual equipment for the conference. A few years before I started working at the department, several of their new projectors were stolen from the conference venue.

The story I was told, from the director and others, was the director of the department held the conference venue door open for a man who had several large bags of equipment. The director was just trying to be helpful, but later analysis put that point as the likely time when the equipment was taken. Unfortunately, there were no security cameras in the venue at that time. Participants, vendors, and staff at the conference now wear ID tags, and the venue has upgraded its security. Had the director asked a few questions, maybe the outcome would've been different.

In any case, if you don't verify authorization then it's like an account with just a username and no password. It's the username and password that are checked against the permissions and authorized access lists. If a system just lets someone based on a username, no real authentication is in place.

Shredding documents

When to shred papers and what documents need to be shredded should be determined by policy and legal requirements.

Documents that no longer need to be stored, which contain personally identifiable information, should be shredded. Some would advise shredding all unneeded paperwork. Personally, I don't go quite that far, but if a paper has a name and address of a family member, the document gets shredded. Generally, if there is any personally identifiable information on the document, or information that could be combined with other documentation to become PII, then it gets shredded.

There are several types of shredders. Most people only really need to know about the three more common types: strip-cut, cross-cut, and micro-cut.

The cheapest, but better-than-nothing, shredders are the strip-cut models. These basically just cut the document into long, narrow strips. A determined person could gather all the strips and potentially piece them back together.

Cross-cut shredders are much more secure than strip-cut ones. The document is cut both vertically and horizontally, resulting in hundreds of very short strips. Only a desperate, and determined, person would even try to put a cross-cut document back together.

Micro-cut shredders are the most secure of these three types. These shredders cut the document into small, confetti-like pieces. While I won't say it's impossible to put the document back together, it is highly unlikely to have it pieced together.

When it comes to how securely the shredder will shred your documents, the smaller the shred size, the more secure.

There is actually an international standard for paper shredding. The German Institute for Standardization defines security standards, and shredders are classified into seven levels (P-1 through P-7), with the higher numbers being more secure. The P-3 rating is for confidential information, while P-4 and higher are for sensitive information requiring more protection.

Strip-cut shredders usually fall into the P-2 level. Depending on the length of the strips, cross-cut shredders may be P-3 or P-4. Micro-cut shredders would be in the P-5 level.

There are several other considerations when it comes to shredders.

First, it's convenient if a shredder can handle more than just paper. Ideally the shredder should be able to destroy plastic cards, like an old credit card, or even a CD or DVD. Shredding a document is more convenient when the shredder can rip through a staple or paper clip than to have to remove these, or risk them binding up the shredder.

The second consideration is how many papers can be fed into the shredder. Low-volume shredders will wear out quickly if you have to shred a lot. But, there's no sense paying a premium for high-capacity shredding if you don't need it.

Safety features are a big consideration. You don't want the shredder to become a hazard. These are some shredder features to consider:

- blade guards
- lockouts to disable the shredder when it's not in use
- slim or angled feed openings to keep fingers from getting caught
- sensors to stop the shredder if a finger gets too close
- an overheating alert
- auto-shutoff in the case of overheating

The speed of the shredder may be another feature to consider. Personal use doesn't necessarily require quick shredding, but if it takes too long, you might end up leaving documents for later and risk documents going missing.

The shred cycle, or duty cycle, might be another consideration, especially if you regularly have a lot of documents to shred. This cycle is how long the shredder can continuously run before it starts to overheat. It includes the shred run time, followed by a cool down. "Run times can be as short as two minutes and cool down times can be as long as 90 minutes depending on the machine."[64]

Locks—windows and doors

In America there are over 2.5 million burglaries reported each year—that's a burglary about every 13 seconds. About 66 percent of those are home break-ins. The rate of property crime for the West, Midwest, and Northeast was about 20 percent in 2013. The South had rate of 37 percent. On a survey of 1,000 people, nearly 1 in 5 said they rarely ever lock their doors, and they never lock their doors when they're home.

The survey also reported 63 percent knowing people who don't lock their doors regularly. It's no wonder 30 percent of burglaries occur through an unlocked door.[65]

The front door is the most likely point of entry. Often the burglar will knock to see is someone is home. Then they'll try the door to see if it's unlocked. Windows on the ground level are the next places they'll try, although they will also look for other options, like garage doors or basement access.[66]

Entry doors should have deadbolts. Patio doors and windows become more difficult to break into with jams. A simple dowel or board in the window or door track can prevent it from opening. If you want to keep the window open, the opening should be no more than 4 inches wide.

If, for some reason, you choose to not lock the door when you are home, and someone you don't know knocks, make yourself known by being loud. Should you decide to answer the door, do it while on the phone (or pretending to be on the phone) with a friend. An intruder is less likely to come in if they believe someone on the phone will know.

The bottom line: lock your doors and windows, especially when you aren't home.

Security systems

Do you want a theft deterrent for your home? Homes that don't have a security system are 2.7 times more likely to be targeted.[67]

A 2013 study into the habits and motivations of burglars surveyed 422 incarcerated male and female burglars and included some of the following findings:

- About 83 percent would determine if there was an alarm first, and 60 percent would find another target if there was an alarm.

- If an alarm was discovered while attempting a burglary, 50 percent would discontinue the attempt, 31 percent would sometimes leave, and only 13 percent would continue.

- Half of those surveyed reported primarily targeting homes, and 31 percent typically targeted commercial establishments.

- Most burglars reported entering through open windows or doors, or they would force a window or door open. Only 1 in 8 said they'd pick the lock or use a key they had gotten.

- About 12 percent reported they would usually plan the burglary in advance, while 41 percent said it was mostly "spur of the moment"; the remaining 37 percent said it varied.

- About 51 percent said the need to get drugs was the motivator behind the burglary, and 37 percent did it for money.[68]

The main targeted valuables are cash, electronics, gold, silver, jewelry, and even guns. Basically, anything that can be sold quickly is of higher value.

So, how do burglaries relate to cybersecurity?

You have two big vulnerabilities where cybersecurity is concerned. Any electronic device that has any of your account information stored on it is a high-value target. Burglars themselves may not be interested in the data on the device, but the person who buys it from them might be.

The other risk factor is any document that someone could use fraudulently. While birth certificates and financial statements may not be the main target, credit and debit cards would be, as well as any other card (including a Social Security card) that might be found in a wallet or purse.

We're not going to discuss all the options for a security system, but as I did spend a summer installing security systems, I have a little familiarity with them. These are some of the many different components you might have as part of a security system:

- alarms—these are the actual sound or alert that is set off
- door and window sensors—these identify whether a door or window is opened
- cameras—the value of seeing without being seen, and even getting recordings and/or images
- motion detectors—these can be on lights or cameras, or even set up as a standalone device to trigger an alarm
- lighting—most people don't consider lighting as part of a security system, but plenty of lighting deters those who prefer to act unseen
- heat sensors—like motion detectors, these can activate a light, camera, alarm, or other device
- glass break detectors—these detect the sound of breaking glass
- timers—like lighting, a timer isn't something usually considered as part of a security system, but they can be used to deter burglars

Don't forget to add the security/alarm system warning sign in the yard or window. It won't scare off all potential burglars, but it will make many of them reconsider your place. Even having a sign when you don't actually have a real security system can act as a deterrent. Unless the intruder knows you don't have a system, many burglars would rather find a less risky target. If you do have a fake alarm sign, you should also add a few other fake components, like a fake camera. If the burglar takes a moment to look around, they might decide the sign could be the real deal.

Safes

There are many kinds of safes and security cases. There are also all kinds of locking options, from simple keys to biometrics. Safes that are either too heavy for a single person to carry, or which are securely attached to the floor or wall, are among the better options to keep valuables from wandering off.

However, unless a burglar knows you won't be home for a long time (like discovering your social media post saying you're on vacation), the average burglar spends 8–12 minutes in the home.[69] They want to get in and out quickly. A locked safe is not as attractive—especially if it's burdensome to carry—as something they can quickly grab and leave with.

Physical security at home

The following are several considerations, recommendations, and suggestions, to help you be more secure at home. Many of these tips may also be applicable to a work environment, particularly small, or at-home, businesses.

Don't post on social media when you are, or will be, on vacation or away from your home.

Don't post pictures of valuable items you have in your home.

Invest in an alarm system. Homes without a security or alarm system are "up to 300 percent more likely to be broken into."[70]

What should be obvious, but doesn't always happen: lock your doors. Remember, 30 percent of all burglaries happen with the offender entering an unlocked door.[71]

Leave some lights, and the television, on when you're gone to make it look like someone might be home.

Don't let your mail accumulate, especially if it's delivered to your door. Go to the United States Postal Service website and request a mail hold. It's easy, and it's free.

Along with a mail hold, don't forget to put any newspaper deliveries on hold.

Shredders are just as important in the home as at work. Make sure any document, including credit card offers with your name and information on them, are shredded.

Important documents should be kept in a secured location.

Let your neighbors know, if you trust them, when you'll be out of town, and ask them to keep watch. Don't forget to return the favor when they're out of town.

Ask your neighbors to remove any flyers that may be hung on your door. A burglar may watch a target to see how long before a flyer gets removed

Consider a house sitter if you'll be gone for an extended period, especially if you can't keep from posting your vacation plans online.

Don't leave trash visible. For example, if you get a new 70-inch ultra-high-definition TV, or any other high-end electronic, the empty box sticking out of the trash is a beacon to thieves that points to your house as a target. Cut up large boxes so it's not obvious to thieves what valuables are inside the house.

If your house isn't in a high-visibility area—maybe it backs up to a forest, is in a cul-de-sac, or even is in the middle of the block—make your home more difficult to access unseen by installing security lighting and high fences.

Your yard gives clues to what's inside. Is the garden really nice? It might indicate there are nice things inside. Are there kids' toys? Then there may be a gaming system.

Leaving a window open, even just a little, can set your home up as a target.

Window air conditioning units are also access points for thieves. It doesn't take much to knock these out and get into the house.

This tip goes for the home and your car: don't leave expensive stuff in plain sight. Some things are hard to hide, like a big TV, but cash and other small valuables are enticing, as they can be quickly grabbed. If a burglar cases your house, you don't want them to see valuables through the windows.

Garage doors are potential entry points. This includes any side or back door into the garage. Make sure these are all locked.

Don't leave spare keys in obvious places, like under the mat or a nearby flower pot. Fake rocks stand out and are noticed by burglars. It's best to not even leave a key anywhere near the front door—not the trim, top, porch light, or any other small hiding place. Burglars will also look for any place a magnetic key holder might stick.[72]

Closing all the blinds and curtains when you leave for vacation, when they are normally open, could indicate you not being home. While open blinds would give full view of what's inside, partially open blinds may let enough light in but still keep things from view and give a burglar pause as to whether you are home or not.

Pet doors are another point of entrance. Even medium-small doors can let a smaller-framed person enter. Even if the person can't physically enter, the pet door may allow the burglar to unlock the door.

Fresh snow can give away your absence by the lack of tire tracks and footprints. Your neighbor could create these tracks and footprints for you.

If you have a glass door, or window in your door, make sure any alarm control pad isn't in view where someone can see if it's set.

Sliding door locks can be easy to open and are too often left unlocked. It's best to have a heavy-duty stick or secondary locking mechanism to keep the door from opening.

Garage keychain remotes are more secure than the bigger remotes. The reason they're more secure is you generally take your keys with you. If a thief steals your garage remote, he has access to the garage, and, likely, the house. Even if you're at work, all it takes is to find the car registration, with your address on it, to discover where the remote will work.

Overgrown grass may also tip off burglars you're out of town.

While lights on in the house at night may be a deterrent, having them on during the day may indicate you're not home. If your house is cased, the unchanging light is a flag that nobody is home. It's better to put your lights on timers, with the lights being off during the daylight hours. The times should be set for lights to go on and off at differing times, to mimic the room being used, and you can even program a late night going to bed.

Overgrown bushes are great hiding places, especially if they're near the house. Keep them trimmed to improve your security.

Don't leave keys near the door, especially if they're within view of a window.

What about guns?

This is a sensitive subject for many. First, I am a proponent of the Second Amendment and feel the right to keep and bear arms is a critical right we have. That said, this is not the venue to discuss the pros or cons of guns. The reality is, each physical location is unique in its environment, neighborhood, and many other factors. So, it's not a simple decision to say "yes" or "no" to including firearms as part of your physical security.

When it comes to cybersecurity, there is little a gun can do to increase your safety. The exception might be if you're trying to prevent someone from taking physical documents or devices that have sensitive information.

Where having a gun is concerned, the biggest factor is to know the local and state laws, and obey those laws. You should also know, and respect, the policies and requests of organizations where firearms are concerned. For example, the state may permit concealed carry, but the law may allow religious, educational, or other private institutions to prohibit the carrying of firearms by non-law enforcement persons.

A few states allow the open carry of firearms, but in our hypersensitive society, just about anyone carrying a firearm is seen as a threat. The wise gun owner who wants to carry a firearm should, where lawful, obtain a concealed carry permit. Being knowledgeable of the laws concerning the use of firearms, particularly where self-defense and security are concerned, is critical.

The short of it is, a gun might keep you from getting robbed. It might deter a thief. But, a gun is not going to keep your account credentials from being phished, and it's not going to stop malware from being installed on your machine if you click a questionable link.

If the other security practices and suggestions are implemented and adapted to your personal needs and conditions, it's probably less likely a gun will be needed in a home or business to protect your personal information. But, the choice and education are up to you.

CHAPTER 15

Paperwork (Hard Copy & Digital)

Paperwork, both hard copies and digital versions, are all part of your identity, or the identify of those in your household or business. For our discussion, "paperwork" can be either in the physical or digital form.

Your biggest consideration when examining the various types of paperwork is whether there is any personally identifiable information (PII) on it. The United States General Services Administration's definition of PII includes "information about a person that contains some unique identifier, including but not limited to name or Social Security Number, from which the identity of the person can be determined."[73] Any PII is not specific to a technology or category of information. Even documents that do not specifically contain PII, if they are combined with other information, may be used to identify an individual.

Categories of paperwork

A lot of paperwork is either classified as PII or has PII on it. The following are some of the different categories of paperwork, along with a few examples.

Vital records

Vital records include driver's licenses, birth certificates, adoption papers, Social Security cards, passports, citizenship papers ("green card" or naturalization documents), marriage licenses, divorce decrees, child custody papers, current military IDs, and military discharges (DD form 214).

Medical information

Medical information can include immunization and other records, prescription information, health insurance cards, powers-of-attorney for health care, and living wills.

Estate planning documents

These can include wills, trusts, and powers-of-attorney.

Financial records

Financial paperwork that has PII includes federal and state tax returns, stock and bond certificates, investment records, brokerage and retirement account information, credit card(s), checking and savings account numbers, and pay stubs.

You should also maintain a list of contact information for credit unions, banks, financial institutions, credit card companies, and financial advisers. In the event of fraud or identity theft, you can quickly contact those who need to know in order to place holds, locks, or simply to monitor accounts.

Insurance policies

Insurance policy paperwork can include homeowners, renters, flood, earthquake, auto, life, health, disability, or long-term care insurance.

Property records

Property records include real estate deeds of trust and mortgage documents; rental agreements or lease; or auto, boat, and RV registration and titles.

Digital assets

Digital asset paperwork can include account and password information for email, social media accounts, financial institutions (banks, credit unions, credit cards, etc.), utilities, and other services.

As you read through these examples, hopefully you realized much of the paperwork may include personal information about others, including members of your household, particularly where spouses may be listed on various accounts. You might also begin to realize how many educational, professional, or other institutions have at least some of your personal information.

As a side note, the documentation listed above is also relevant to emergency preparations. Securing PII is comparable to preparing for a possible emergency, which, in the context of this book, is to protect against identity theft.

Securing paperwork

Physically securing any hard copies needs to be a priority. How you do it depends on your circumstances.

If you are receiving physical copies of statements in the mail, you should consider possible security risks, such as the mail being intercepted or read. It is not difficult for someone to take mail from the mailbox. Even though it's a federal offense, there is no login information for the mailbox and no access log for who opened it. So, it's very difficult to know if something was lost or stolen.

To help prevent the loss or theft of documentation, you might consider, whenever possible, to receive documentation digitally, usually through email. However, you still need to take steps to make sure your devices store the information securely. This includes encrypting the digital files.

Some people will scan and save digital copies of vital and important paperwork. These copies are used as backups, particularly in case of emergencies.

In you do keep digital copies of your important documents, those files should be encrypted.

Access information for digital assets

In recent years, access to digital assets has become more of a consideration. What happens if you are no longer able to access your digital assets? Perhaps you're incapacitated. Or, maybe you've passed on from this life and your significant other, or business partner, needs to access your digital assets.

Some people mistakenly believe that when they die, their digital assets won't have any effect on others. However, any compromised account— whether the account owner is alive or dead—can affect others. The account can be used to find other accounts or contact information. If the other accounts include financial institutions, then financial theft could be the result, which directly affects the spouse and/or family members.

In any case, what is your plan for your digital assets?

For some people, account information is referenced in a will—maybe to a safe where the actual information is stored.

Others maintain a password manager with their spouse. Then, as a backup, the master password for the password manager is what is provided to a trusted person or put into a safe.

There have been instances where the spouse who takes care of all the finances dies, and the surviving spouse has no clue where to go or what to do.

I personally know of a similar event. In this case, a family member passed, and the spouse had died years earlier. There was no record, or accounting, of assets. Physical assets had to be tediously tracked down. Add to that, there was no digital account information. Not even a list of accounts. Weeks' worth of work was put into trying to identify assets and accounts. The sad thing is, the family will probably never know if they missed an account somewhere.

CHAPTER 16

Securing Your Identity

Money is the primary motivator for criminal activity on the web. But there are a lot of ways for the cybercriminal to get money besides stealing it from your bank account. One very common way, which we have referred to throughout this book, is to steal and then sell your information, your identity.

Because your information security relies on you, you need to be aware of various aspects of identity theft, including where your information is vulnerable, how to better protect it, ways to monitor for identity theft, and what to do in the event of that theft. This information is not just applicable to you but to others you know as well.

Identity thieves steal personal information through a variety of ways. Some of their methods include

- digging through trash and other places, including documents lying around, looking for information like credit card numbers, account numbers, Social Security numbers, and other personal information;
- retrieving information from discarded, lost, or stolen computers, phones, wallets, or other items;
- using radio frequency identification readers to steal information from checks, credit and debit cards, passports, driver's licenses, or Social Security cards. They may use skimmers to swipe information from card readers and then create a new card;
- installing malware or spyware to steal information from computers and other devices;

- hacking computer networks and databases, or infiltrating organizations, to steal large amounts of personal and/or valuable information; and
- acting as a trusted individual or organization (social engineering) to obtain personal and/or financial information through mail, phone, messaging, and email.

Some of the warning signs of identity theft or fraud include

- bills that don't arrive when you expect them to;
- receiving unexpected credit cards or account statements;
- receiving denials of credit you didn't apply for;
- receiving calls or letters regarding purchases you didn't make;
- charges on financial statements you don't recognize; and
- incorrect, inaccurate, and unrecognized information, such as accounts or addresses, on your credit reports.

Besides keeping your accounts safe, you need to monitor and protect your credit as well. Where finances are concerned your credit score, which is computed using various factors, is one of the most important determinants. With a good score, you're more likely to get better interest rates. A bad score may not even get you a loan.

Free credit reports

Your credit report can affect credit rates, such as for a mortgage, credit card approvals, rentals, and possibly on a job application. You need to be aware of what is on your credit report and regularly check it to make sure the information is accurate. Make sure you recognize the information on the report, including

- personally identifiable information—names, addresses, Social Security number and
- accounts and loans.

There are a lot of sites promising free credit reports, but you need to be wary of these sites.

Federal law allows you to get one free copy of your credit report every 12 months from each credit reporting company. The only official site directed by federal law to provide free reports is https://www.annualcreditreport.com/index.action.

Credit freeze

It used to be that requesting a credit freeze on your account would cost you—not a lot, but you would need to pay each credit rating agency to freeze your credit, and many states had an associated fee. The combined fees could add up.

After the Equifax data breach in 2017, there was a lot of outcry from the public regarding credit freezes, and Congress actually listened and did something about it.

Beginning September 21, 2018, credit freezes, also known as a security freeze, are free. According to the law, you can freeze and unfreeze your credit file for free.

You can also request credit freezes for your children who are under 16 years old. "And if you are someone's guardian, conservator or have a valid power of attorney, you can get a free freeze for that person, too."[63]

A credit freeze is not a credit lock, although they are similar. The biggest difference is a credit lock will likely have a monthly fee, and it's probably what the agency will try to convince you to have. If you want the free option, you need the freeze, not the lock.

When you request a credit freeze, which you need to do with each agency, the credit agency is supposed to place the freeze within one business day, if the request was made online or by phone. If the request was mailed, the agency has three business days after receiving the request to freeze the account.

When you request the freeze to be lifted, by phone or online, the agency is to lift the freeze within one hour. Temporary freeze lifts are also available for free.

The new law also increased the length of time for credit fraud alerts.

With a fraud alert, businesses are supposed to check with you before a new account is opened. It used to be the fraud alert would only last for 90 days, and then you'd have to request it again. Now fraud alerts last a year, and they are still free.

Active duty alerts are still available for members of the military. These alerts place a one-year fraud alert your account, and the reporting agencies are supposed to remove your name from their prescreened marketing lists.

Contact information for the three main credit bureaus can be found on the   identitytheft.gov   website,   at https://www.identitytheft.gov/creditbureaucontacts.

Protecting against identity fraud

Besides creating fraudulent accounts, or using stolen bank information or credit cards, there are other types of identity theft:

- tax ID theft, where someone uses your Social Security number to falsely file a tax return
- medical ID theft, which occurs when your Medicare ID or health insurance number is stolen and the thief uses it to get medical services or submit fake bills
- social ID theft happens when someone uses your name and photos to create a fake social media account

The following tips are from the U.S. government's identify theft site, https://www.usa.gov/identity-theft. You'll probably notice similarity to other tips and suggestions listed in this book.

- Secure your Social Security number. Don't carry your Social Security card in your wallet or purse, and only give out your Social Security number when it's absolutely necessary.

- Don't share your personal information just because someone asks for it. It may sound obvious, but some people don't think twice about sharing a birthdate, Social Security number, or even financial account information.

- Pick up your mail every day. If you're going to be gone for several days, place a mail hold.

- Pay attention to your billing cycles, and if bills or statements are late, be sure to contact the sender. Missing bills can be a red flag.

- Enable security features on your phone.

- Update the file sharing and firewall settings on your computer or other device, especially when you're on a public Wi-Fi network. Use a virtual private network (VPN) if you're using public Wi-Fi.

- Regularly review the account statements from your financial institutions. Verify transactions, comparing receipts with the statements. Look for unauthorized transactions.

- Be sure to shred receipts, credit card offers, account statements, expired credit cards, and other documentation that contains personal information to prevent dumpster divers from getting your information.

- Securely store your personal information.

- Install firewalls and anti-malware software on your computers.

- Create secure passphrases. Change your passphrase if the organization has a data breach.

- Review your credit reports yearly, and check for accounts that you did not open.

- Freeze your credit files with each of the credit reporting organizations.

To help prevent tax identity theft, follow these recommendations:

- File your income taxes early, before a thief can file in your name.
- Watch for an IRS letter or notice that states
    - more than one tax return was filed using your Social Security number;
    - you owe additional tax, have a tax refund offset, or have had collection actions against you for a year you didn't file a return; or
    - you receive wages from an employer you don't know.
- Don't reply or click on links in any suspicious email, text, or social media messages.

With regards to protecting yourself from medical identity theft, you should also protect yourself in these ways:

- Protect not only your Social Security number but also your Medicare and other health insurance identification numbers. Only give them to approved providers.
- Review your insurance explanation of benefits or Medicare Summary Notice, and check that claims match the services received. Report any questionable charges to Medicare or your health insurance provider.
- Request and review a copy of your medical records for errors, inaccuracies, and conditions that you don't have.

Protecting minors' credit

Those of us with children are also responsible for protecting their credit.

A lot of parents choose to get Social Security numbers for their children, frequently for tax purposes. Regardless of the reason, if a child has a

Social Security number issued, they are vulnerable to identify theft. Even as a baby or young child.

Identity thieves like using Social Security numbers of children because in most cases it will be years before the theft is discovered.

The Federal Trade Commission has more information about child identity theft at https://www.consumer.ftc.gov/articles/0040-child-identity-theft.

Watch for warning signs

There are some big tip offs a child's personal information is being misused. Some red flags include if you or your child

- receive notice from the IRS that the child has not paid income taxes or that the child's Social Security number was used on another tax return;
- get collection calls or bills for services or products that weren't received; or
- get denied government benefits because your child's Social Security number is being used on another account to receive benefits.

Get a credit report for your child

As mentioned in an earlier section, credit freezes for minors under the age of 16 can be requested from each of the credit reporting agencies. Each credit bureau has its own instructions; contact information can be found at https://www.identitytheft.gov/Info-Lost-or-Stolen under the "Children's personal information" section. As of this writing, the following information is listed on the site:

Equifax
https://www.equifax.com/personal/credit-report-services
phone: 1-800-685-1111

Experian
http://www.experian.com/help
phone: 1-888-397-3742

Transunion
http://www.transunion.com/credit-help
Phone: 1-888-909-8872

In most cases, children will not have a credit report unless someone is using their credit information. You can request a credit report by asking each credit agency to check its records. Each bureau has its own instructions for these requests:

https://www.ai.equifax.com/CreditInvestigation/home/MinorChild.html

https://www.experian.com/fraudalert

https://www.transunion.com/personal-credit/credit-disputes/fraud-victim-resources/child-identity-theft-inquiry-form.page

If there is a credit report, you can check it for fraudulent accounts and act to remove them.

Additionally, some states offer credit protection for minors through a state program. For example, in Utah the Utah Attorney General's Child Identity Protection (CIP) program allows parents or guardians to enroll their child's information through CIP. The information is entered into a fraud prevention program and added to a high-risk fraud database until the child's 17th birthday.

Repair damage found

Contact any companies where the fraud occurred, and inform them the fraudulent account was opened using the child's identity. Request the account be closed, and have them send you a letter stating the child isn't liable. You may need to send a letter explaining the child is a minor who cannot legally enter into contracts; a copy of the child's birth certificate may need to be included.

You should contact the credit bureaus and request that they remove any fraudulent accounts from your child's credit report. They may also need a similar letter, explaining the child is a minor who can't enter into contracts.

You may want to request a credit freeze on the child's credit file until they are old enough to use it. The freeze restricts the account, making it more difficult to be used by identify thieves.

Identity theft should be reported to the Federal Trade Commission by going to https://www.identitytheft.gov/ or calling 877-ID-THEFT.

Preventing fraud

Prevention is the best form of protection. It is your defense against attackers. The whole goal of this book is to help you better protect yourself and those you care about from those who want your personal information.

Just like documents with your own information, all paper and electronic records that have your child's personal information need to be stored securely. Any documents with personal information on them should be shredded before being thrown away.

Your child's Social Security number should not be shared unless you know and trust the other party and have found out how it will be protected. If possible, another identifier or just the last four digits of the Social Security number should be used.

Be aware of other situations that could potentially put identities at risk:

- an adult in the household wanting to use the child's identity to "start over"
- loss of a wallet, purse, or paperwork that has the child's Social Security number information
- a break-in at your home
- a notification from the school, doctor's office, or other organization that your child's information was affected by a data breach

Limiting the risks of child identity theft

There are laws designed to help protect personal information. In educational environments, the Federal Family Educational Rights and Privacy Act (FERPA) protects the privacy of student records. FERPA gives the parents or guardians of school-age children the right to opt out of sharing contact or other directory information with third parties, which can include other families.

If you have children in school, there are some recommendations from the Federal Trade Commission about protecting your child's identity.

Find out who has access to your child's information, and verify that the records are securely stored.

Ask about the school's directory information policy. This information may include your child's name, address, date of birth, telephone number, email address, and even photo. You have the right to opt out of the release of this information to third parties. If you do opt out, do it in writing and keep a copy. If you don't opt out, the information may be available to the child's class, school, and, possibly, the general public, depending on the school's directory policy.

Forms will likely come home with the child, through the mail or email, asking for personal information. Find out how your child's information will be used, where it will be shared, and who will have access to it. Terms like "personally identifiable information," "directory information," and "opt out" can help you identify whether or not the information should be shared.

Some schools distribute surveys and instructional materials to students. Under the Protection of Pupil Rights Amendment (PPRA) (20 U.S.C. § 1232h; 34 CFR Part 98), programs that receive funding from the U.S. Department of Education must "protect the rights of parents and students in two ways:

> "It seeks to ensure that schools and contractors make instructional materials available for inspection by parents if those materials will be used in connection with an ED-funded survey, analysis, or evaluation in which their children participate; and

> "It seeks to ensure that schools and contractors obtain written parental consent before minor students are required to participate in any ED-funded survey, analysis, or evaluation that reveals information" such as political affiliations; mental or psychological problems; illegal, anti-social, self-incriminating, and demeaning behavior; sex behavior and attitudes; and other information.

More information about PPRA can be found at https://www2.ed.gov/policy//gen/guid/fpco/ppra/index.html.

Under FERPA, schools are required to send annual notices explaining your rights, including your right to

- review and inspect your child's educational records,
- approve the disclosure of personal information, and
- request the correction of errors.

You should also consider other programs that happen at the school, such as sports and music, which may not be formally sponsored by the school. Some of these programs may have websites where the children's names and pictures are displayed. Read the privacy policies to find out if, and how, your child's information will be used and shared.

There are other laws and regulations that also involve the security of your child's information. For example, in healthcare, the Health Insurance Portability and Accountability Act (HIPAA) has regulations in place to secure and protect the privacy of your information, as well as the personal information of your children, in healthcare environments.

We won't go into details about any more of the laws; just know there are some regulations designed to protect your data, and more are being considered and crafted. However, because identity thieves don't care about the laws, you still need to be vigilant in securing the identities of your children.

When it's close to your child's 16th birthday, it's a good idea to check the child's credit report. If there is an error or fraud, you should have time to work on correcting it. If you placed a credit freeze, you'll need to lift it before the child can apply for any new credit.

Reporting identity theft

Identity theft should be reported to the Federal Trade Commission at https://www.identitytheft.gov/ or by phone at 1-877-438-4338.

Medical identity fraud should be reported to the appropriate agency. If it's Medicare fraud, report it to Medicare's fraud office, https://oig.hhs.gov/fraud/report-fraud/. You can also contact the U.S. Department of Health and Human Services' Inspector General at 1-800-447-8477.

Tax Identity theft should be reported to the Internal Revenue Service, after reporting it to the Federal Trade Commission. This IRS link is to the current Taxpayer Guide to Identity Theft, https://www.irs.gov/newsroom/taxpayer-guide-to-identity-theft.

You need to also report identity theft to other applicable organizations, such as

- credit reporting agencies,
- financial institutions,
- retailers and other companies, and
- your state consumer protection offices or attorney general. You can look up state consumer protection offices at https://www.usa.gov/state-consumer.

If the identity theft results from a stay in a nursing home or long-term care facility, the theft should also be reported to the National Long-Term Care Ombudsman Resource Center, https://theconsumervoice.org/get_help.

What to do when a data breach happens

It's practically a guarantee some of your information has been stolen at some time. It may be from old website accounts you have forgotten about and haven't used in years. At some point more of your data will be compromised as part of a data breach. It's not a matter of if, but when. And when it does, you need to be ready to act.

Find out the extent of the damage. Start with these actions:

- Confirm with the organization that a breach occurred and whether your information was compromised.
- Find out what information was stolen and how the information was stored. Were passwords salted and hashed? Was the information encrypted? Was any information in cleartext?
- Was your Social Security number exposed and/or any other personally identifiable information (PII) stolen?

Hopefully the passwords were salted and hashed with a strong algorithm, and any other information was encrypted. If it was, you have a bit more breathing room. If it wasn't, you need to get moving with further protective measures.

Change your passwords. This is particularly applicable to the site(s) that were breached and any sites that may be referenced in your profile on the breached site(s). For example, in your profile at the breached site you will likely have an email listed. It would be a good idea to change the password for that email. This is especially true if you happen to be reusing the same password. If your email has been hacked, consider all the messages you've received from other sites, like banks, ecommerce sites, credit card companies, etc. If you've been using the same password for any (or worse, all) of those other sites, the hacker will be able to identify those sites from the email and access them (because you used the same password). Your only safe course of action: change your passwords.

Change any security questions and answers you may have set up that are related to the compromised account.

Use a password manager to help you create and protect your passwords.

If any financial (bank account information, credit cards, etc.), government identification (tax information, Social Security number, driver's license, etc.), or other personally identifiable information was part of the data breach, you should contact the credit bureaus to advise them you've been a victim of identity theft and to place a fraud alert on your file. If you haven't done so already, request a credit freeze.

If your driver's license number was stolen, you will need to contact your state's agency over driver's licensing. In many states this may be the Division of Motor Vehicles.

Call your banks and credit card companies to lock your affected account and prevent new transactions. Delaying this by even a few minutes can allow the criminals to rack up thousands of dollars of damages.

Monitor your financial accounts. Even if you have auto-pay, you should regularly log in to each account where financial transactions occur and review those transactions. Make sure you can identify each transaction.

You may be advised to file a police report and a Federal Trade Commission report. However, every event and the extent of damages should be included in these reports, and you may not know them immediately. So, while these reports would be good to file, you may need to wait to get more information. Just don't delay too long.

Make sure you document everything: who you talk to and when, and everything you do.

Get a copy of your credit report. You can use one of your three annual reports for this request. The idea is to identify anything unusual and to include that with the police and Federal Trade Commission reports.

Enable (opt in to) two-factor authentication, if it's available, for the breached site as well as all other sites that offer it.

File your taxes early. Your goal is to beat any fraudsters attempting to commit tax refund identity theft using your Social Security number.

The IdentityTheft.gov site has recommendations for what to do when your information is lost or exposed for the following:

- Social Security number
- online login or password
- debit or credit card number
- bank account information
- driver's license information
- children's personal information

Access the site at https://www.identitytheft.gov/Info-Lost-or-Stolen.

CHAPTER 17

Data Privacy and Security

From 2016 through 2018, "more than 11.7 billion records and over 11 Terabytes of data were leaked or stolen in publicly disclosed incidents."[74] We briefly mentioned the size of a terabyte earlier in this book, but it's hard to grasp how much information it is. For a comparison, 11 terabytes are comparable to five billion single-space pages of text. At 300 pages per book, that's over 16.5 million books.

The information in these records leaked or stolen records include personally identifiable information (such as Social Security numbers, addresses, phone numbers, bank and payment card information, passport data, etc.), other account information (usernames, passwords, email, etc.), and personal health records, which may include medical information along with insurance information, tests, and laboratory results.

The question isn't *if* some of your personal data is part of those leaked or stolen records; the question is more *what* of your personal information has been leaked or stolen. Because of the increasing security and privacy concerns, new laws are being proposed and enacted to help you better protect and control your data.

As we reach the end of your security awareness briefing, it'd be good for you to know there are laws in place, at least in some countries and some states, that are supposed to help you keep some control of your data stored by organizations. But, you also need to be proactive in protecting your information.

Of course, there are laws against the unlawful access and use of computing and network systems. And laws that try to protect your data privacy and ensure adequate security measures are in place. However, a law doesn't keep the cybercriminal from trying to steal your data, and the unfortunate reality is, it's extremely difficult to precisely identify the actual perpetrators of cybercrimes. Few cybercriminals are caught and convicted for most data breaches that happen. Most of the time, the best that law enforcement agencies can do is point a finger to the most likely culprits, which are often from an international origin, like Russia, China, or Korea.

That said, in 2018, the European Union (EU) passed a law that became enforceable in all the EU countries and is known as the General Data Protection Regulation, or GDPR.

GDPR

Have you noticed an increased number of privacy notifications in your email, particularly since the summer of 2018?

Have you noticed an increased number of sites informing you the site uses cookies, and asking you to approve the use of cookies?

While privacy and cookie notices might be annoying, they are results of the GDPR. The GDPR is directly applicable to citizens of the EU, and it attempts to take back control of personal data from corporations and return it to the individuals. Personal data includes photos, emails, bank and financial information, social media updates, location details, medical information, and computer/device information that can identify device location, such as the IP address. Because site cookies often contain device information, companies have to ask permission before a cookie can be used.

Every company that is established in the EU must be compliant with the GDPR, even if they store or process their data in a non-EU location.

And any company that offers goods and/or services to citizens of the EU must also be compliant.

Although local American companies aren't concerned with the GDPR, big international ones are. These includes companies like Facebook, Microsoft, and Google. Many of these companies have decided to implement the GDPR-required changes across the board, meaning those of us not in the EU have been able to see some benefits to better control our data.

If the company is compliant with GDPR requirements, there are eight rights you get with regards to your data.

1. You have the right to request access to your personal data and ask how the company will be using your data. The company must provide a copy of the personal data, free of charge.
2. With the right to be forgotten, you can withdraw your consent for a company to use your data, and even request the data to be deleted.
3. The right to data portability allows you to transfer your data from one service provider to another in a common, machine-readable format.
4. You have the right to be informed of what data is being collected and how that data will be used, and you have to opt in with consent freely given rather than implied.
5. You also have the right to have information corrected. If you discover any information that is out-of-date, incomplete, or incorrect, you can have it corrected.
6. The right to restrict processing allows your record to remain, but you can request your data not be used in processing.
7. The right to object allows you to stop the processing of your data for direct marketing, and the processing must stop as soon as the request is received.
8. The eighth right is to be notified of a data breach that compromises your personal data. After becoming aware of the

breach, the company has to inform you within 72 hours if your data was compromised. If your data wasn't compromised, you may not get a notification.

Even though the GDPR regulation is in the EU, it affects most users. It's also good to know because there are similar regulations being considered and passed at the state level in the United States.

Increased privacy coming

In June 2018, California passed the California Consumer Privacy Act of 2018. Although it's not as strict as the GDPR, it will become the toughest data privacy law in America. The legislation takes effect in 2020.

Because of California's law, we will see a trickle effect. Companies that may not do business in the EU but have a presence or have customers in California will likely have to comply with the law.

The rest of the states will likely consider updated privacy and security laws over the coming years. This will be especially true if the United States Congress fails to pass updated, and more comprehensive, data privacy laws.

Disposal of devices

At some point you will likely replace your computer, phone, or other device. What do you do with the old device before you hand it off to a child, donate it, or sell it?

The most important thing you should do before getting rid of the device is to erase your personal information from it.

First you should, for a last time, back up all your data to another location—computer, cloud storage, flash drive, etc. Check your backup and compare it to the files on the device. If there is additional storage in the device, like a micro SD card on a phone, remove the storage from the device.

You might also want to go into each browser you regularly use and export the information in the browser, such as your favorites and bookmarks. You can import this information into the browser on another device. If this is too much work, you might be able to log in to the browser (create an account, if you don't have one already) and sync various settings. Then, on another device, you can log in to the same browser and still have access to your tabs, favorites, bookmarks, and whatever else has been synced.

If the device is on a device management account, like "Find My iPhone" or "Find my Android," you need to remove the device from the account. If it's not removed, the new owner won't be able to do much with it.

If you aren't completely wiping the hard drive or performing a full factory reset on the device, make sure you go into the settings of every browser on the device and delete your saved information, history, etc. and reset the browser. It's better to securely wipe the hard drive of a computer, or to have a complete factory reset done on a mobile device.

Securely erase your data from the device. Some might call this clearing, wiping, or removing your data. This is more than just sending things to the trash, since it's easy to recover data from the trash, and emptying the trash doesn't securely erase your data.

Do you remember the comparison of a computer to an office, and the hard drive to a file cabinet? Well, your data and files are given what amounts to a file index so the OS can find them. Trashing a file puts that index reference into the trash folder, where it can be easily recovered. Removing/deleting an item from the trash is like throwing away the index tab of the file. The file itself is still on the hard drive— only the index reference has been tossed. To the computer, the space where the file is located is considered empty and available. Eventually the space will be overwritten with new data. However, until the space is overwritten, recovery software might still be able to access the "deleted" files.

What needs to happen is for your files to be securely deleted. There is software, even some free software, that can do the job for you. Some operating systems have the option to perform a secure delete.

After your personal data is cleared from the device, it should be reset to factory condition.

For computers, the best option is to completely wipe the hard drive. Drive wiping software that loads from a CD/DVD or USB drive is usually used to erase, and write meaningless data over, the hard drive.

Another option, if the hard drive or storage is removeable, is to take out the drive and keep it, instead of getting rid of it with the device. Instead of wiping a hard drive, I have kept some old drives as backups and gotten rid of the rest of the hardware. The hard drive could also be destroyed to eliminate the possibility of recovering data.

Remember, before you get rid of the device, make sure your data, as well as anyone else's stored on the device, is erased. Ideally, your data was previously encrypted on the device. Then, after erasing the data, if someone located the deleted files, the files would be meaningless gibberish because of the encryption.

Whenever possible, you should recycle electronics instead of trashing them, although recycling usually isn't as easy as putting the device in a curbside recycling bin. You can check with the retailer of the new device you purchased to see if they offer recycling, contact the recycling center, or do an internet search to find nearby electronics recycling. Just make sure any personal information is cleared from the device first.

Don't get comfortable

Just because there are, and will be, more data privacy and security regulations in place does not mean you should relax in your personal efforts. You still need to protect your data as well as the data of those in your care. You still need to use secure practices and to exercise caution, especially online.

As mentioned at the beginning, my purpose has been education and awareness. The goal was not to make you a cybersecurity expert. Rather, the intent is to give you a basis of understanding. Hopefully you won't feel clueless and lost when some security or computer term is mentioned in the future, where you just nod your head but have no idea what was just said.

With technology evolving so quickly, it's difficult to keep up. The constant change makes a lot of people uncomfortable, and many feel intimidated by the unfamiliar.

However, you can still apply the security principles discussed as technology changes. Here's a review of some of those principles:

- Keep your device OS up-to-date.
- Have an anti-malware solution installed, and keep it updated.
- Use strong, and long, passphrases.
- Use a password manager.
- Use encryption on sensitive data.
- Change default account names and passwords.
- Maintain regular backups of your data.
- Keep a data backup that isn't constantly connected to your device.
- Be careful with unsolicited emails.
- Be aware of social engineering tactics.
- Adjust social media privacy settings so you're not sharing everything with everyone.

- Don't overshare on social media.
- Keep your personally identifiable information secure.

Some final words

As we increasingly move into a digital economy, and our devices and screens become ever more in-our-faces, we need to remember that not everyone in the virtual world is looking out for our best interests.

If you've ever felt that some people, maybe even you, are addicted to a device, like a smartphone app, it's not far from the truth. Applications are designed to engage you—to make it hard to put it down. But, as we become more involved virtually, are we losing a sense of reality?

It's easy to automatically grant permissions and give up your privacy, and even security, for the convenience, entertainment, and ease promised by various applications. Most people don't give it much thought. Are you trading your security and privacy for immediate satisfaction, ease, comfort, and convenience?

As you consider the many devices you use, and the numerous applications on them, what can you do now to make your data more secure? Because it can be overwhelming with where to start, start with the list we began with, plus one additional item:

- Make sure your computer has an up-to-date operating system.
- Make sure your anti-malware application is running and updated.
- Examine the passwords you're regularly using, and change them, if needed, so they are more secure.
- Create backups of your data from all your devices.
- Set up two-factor authentication wherever you can.

Then go on to other areas, such as securing mobile devices and other "things" connected to the internet, including your local network.

Throughout the process, work on better physical security and securely handling potentially sensitive paperwork. If you have children, start teaching them to become more security conscious. Becoming more secure begins with awareness.

While it'd be great to get it all done immediately, cybersecurity takes time; for most of us, it can only be done a little at a time. However, it's also good it takes time because it keeps us more aware of potential security issues. There are those who start out security minded, but after doing a few things they fall into complacency and stop the continual effort. This is like updating your computer and anti-malware to the latest versions and then not doing it again. Eventually those versions will become seriously outdated again.

Being security minded is a continuous process.

I'm hoping you learned something, or at least have a greater awareness of the security and privacy risks that lurk everywhere. If you have children, you need to help them increase their security awareness. Share what you've learned with others.

I appreciate your time in reading my book. I've attempted to cover as many security bases as I could in a relatively short time. No doubt I could have spent more time in some areas, maybe less in others, and I may have missed something. Best practices continue to evolve, and technology is rapidly changing. However, many of the basics we've covered will likely continue to be emphasized in the effort to help you maintain your security and privacy.

Be safe in your virtual and physical worlds.

Top Factors in Data Breaches

The information in this section comes from Verizon's 2018 Data Breach Investigations Report (DBIR), 11th edition. The reporting year is based on incidents in 2017. There were over 53,000 incidents, with 2,216 of those being confirmed data breaches. Most of those you probably didn't hear about in the news. You should also know this report is primarily business security incidents.

The DBIR is about 68 pages long, and only a few of the highlights are presented here. If you're interested, the report can be accessed from this website:

> https://enterprise.verizon.com/resources/reports/DBIR_2018_Report.pdf

The terms "incident" and "breach" are used. The DBIR defines incidents as "a security event that compromises the integrity, confidentiality or availability of an information asset." A breach is "an incident that results in the confirmed disclosure—not just potential exposure—of data to an unauthorized party."

Who are the actors behind the data breaches?

- 73% were perpetrated by an external source.
- 28% involved internal actors.
- 50% were carried out by criminal groups.
- 12% involved nation-state or state-affiliated groups.

How were the breaches carried out?

- 48% involved hacking.

- 30% included malware.
- 17% involved errors.
- 17% were social attacks.
- 12% were misused privilege.
- 11% involved physical actions.

Who are the victims of the data breaches?

- 58% were small businesses.
- 14% were in the public sector.
- 15% were accommodation and food services.
- 24% were healthcare organizations.

Some of the other common factors of the breaches are:

- 49% of non-point-of-sale malware were installed from malicious email.
- 76% had financial motivations.
- 13% were to gain strategic advantage or espionage.
- 68% took months or longer to discover.

Top 10 incidents

The following table is out of 30,362 reported incidents.

Table 4: Actions causing top 10 incidents.

# of Incidents	Action Causing Incident
21,409	Denial of Service—DoS (hacking)
3,740	Loss (error)
1,192	Phishing (social)
973	Mis-delivery (error)
787	Ransomware (malware)
631	Command and control of the infected system (malware)
424	Use of stolen credentials (hacking)
318	RAM scraper (malware)
233	Privilege abuse (misuse)
221	Use of backdoor or command and control of the infected system (hacking)

You may note the number of incidents involving ransomware, but, in the following table, ransomware isn't an action causing breaches. This is because in most ransomware cases, the data is never stolen. The data is encrypted so it's unusable to the victim, unless they pay for the decryption.

Top 10 breaches

The following table is out of 1,799 confirmed data breaches.

Table 5: Actions causing top 10 data breaches.

# of Breaches	Action Causing Breach
399	Use of stolen credentials (hacking)
312	RAM scraper (malware)
236	Phishing (social)
201	Privilege abuse (misuse)
187	Mis-delivery (error)
148	Use of backdoor or command and control of the infected system (hacking)
123	Theft (physical)
117	command and control of the infected system (malware)
115	Backdoor (malware)
114	Pretexting (social)

Top data compromised

The next table is from 2,037 data breaches.

Table 6: Categories of data compromised in top breaches.

# of Breaches	Data Compromised
730	Personal
563	Payment
505	Medical
221	Credentials
154	Internal
137	Secrets
62	System
60	Bank
24	Classified

Most-targeted Industries - 2018

The following information is from IBM Security's X-Force Threat Intelligence Index 2019.

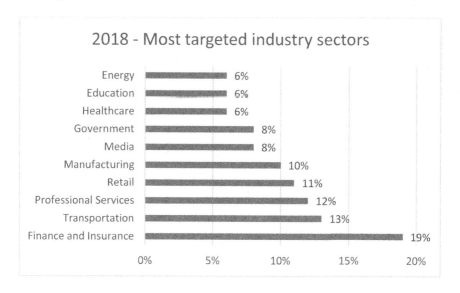

Figure 22: 2018 Most-targeted industries in 2018.

Cybercriminals are after anything that offers financial gain. Banking and payment card information, personally identifiable information, loyalty-rewards accounts, and proprietary information are some of the data that can be either directly profitable or sold for a profit.

It's likely you have information stored with companies and organizations in several of the industry sectors.

100 of the Worst Passwords

100. biteme	66. blahblah	32. baseball
99. 1992	65. mercedes	31. passw0rd
98. london	64. corvette	30. shadow
97. soccer	63. computer	29. freedom
96. william	62. cheese	28. bailey
95. querty	61. ferrari	27. 121212
94. liverpool	60. starwars	26. zxcvbnm
93. pussy	59. 1qaz2wsx	25. qwerty123
92. admin123	58. andrea	24. password1
91. whatever	57. lakers	23. donald
90. dallas	56. andrew	22. aa123456
89. hockey	55. 12341234	21. charlie
88. test	54. matthew	20. !@#$%^&*
87. zaq1zaq1	53. robert	19. 654321
86. 1q2w3e	52. 1234	18. monkey
85. aaaaaa	51. sophie	17. 123123
84. killer	50. pepper	16. football
83. bandit	49. joshua	15. abc123
82. ashley	48. tigger	14. 666666
81. cookie	47. 55555	13. welcome
80. merlin	46. jordan	12. admin
79. trustno1	45. solo	11. princess
78. 1991	44. abcdef	10. iloveyou
77. ranger	43. letmein	9. qwerty
76. chelsea	42. ginger	8. sunshine
75. banana	41. jessica	7. 1234567
74. jennifer	40. 222222	6. 111111
73. 1990	39. harley	5. 12345
72. amanda	38. george	4. 12345678
71. 1989	37. summer	3. 123456789
70. hunter	36. thomas	2. password
69. nicole	35. hannah	1. 123456
68. hello	34. daniel	
67. maverick	33. buster	

The 100 worst passwords of 2018, taken from https://www.teamsid.com/100-worst-passwords/.

Works Cited

To help the book flow easier, I used endnotes to reference the works cited. Full reference information is in the bibliography.

1. Frankenfield, 2019
2. Savoie, 2012
3. Fractional CISO, 2019
4. Verger, 2017
5. Bursztein, 2015
6. Bursztein, 2015
7. Bonneau, Bursztein, Caron, Jackson, & Williamson, 2015
8. Bonneau, Bursztein, Caron, Jackson, & Williamson, 2015
9. Hampson, 2019
10. Hampson, 2019
11. Giusti, 2018
12. Graham, 2017
13. Phillips, 10 Basic Encryption Terms Everyone Should Know and Understand, 2018
14. Mort & Foss, 2016
15. Brumley, 2019
16. IBM Security, 2019
17. Calyptix, 2018
18. Monnappa, 2018
19. Verizon, 2018
20. Ponemon Institute, 2018
21. Monnappa, 2018
22. IBM Security, 2019
23. Fortney, 2019
24. Morgan, 2016
25. Dayaratna, 2018
26. Morgan, 2016
27. Brumley, 2019
28. Department of Homeland Security
29. Verizon, 2018
30. Segarra, 2018

31. Verizon, 2018
32. IBM Security, 2019
33. IBM Security, 2019
34. Rouse, 2018
35. Verizon, 2018
36. Leyden, 2003
37. Université du Luxembourg, 2016
38. Chokey, 2019
39. Fletcher, 2018
40. La Rosa, 2018
41. Morris, 2018
42. Morris, 2018
43. ABC News, 2014
44. National Cybersecurity and Communications Integration Center, 2015
45. Reed, 2016
46. Holpuch, 2013
47. Aji, Riadi, & Lutfhi, 2017
48. Middlebrook, 2016
49. Thomas, 2018
50. Royal College of Paediatricss and Child Health, 2019
51. Hill, 2018
52. Brown, 2017
53. Coughlan, 2018
54. Crane, 2019
55. IBM Security, 2019
56. IBM Security, 2019
57. Ponemon Institute, 2018
58. Statista, 2019
59. Boodaei, 2011
60. Goodin, 2015
61. Cervantes, 2015
62. FCC, 2018
63. Smith, 2018
64. Herrick, 2017
65. Eyewitness Surveillance, 2017
66. DeMille, 2019
67. DeMille, 2019
68. Roberson, 2013
69. DeMille, 2019
70. Eyewitness Surveillance, 2017
71. Eyewitness Surveillance, 2017

72. Erickson, n.d.
73. U.S. General Services Administration, 2014
74. IBM Security, 2019

Bibliography

ABC News. (2014, December 23). *abc7news.com*. Retrieved from Burglars use social media to find next victims: https://abc7news.com/travel/burglars-use-social-media-to-find-next-victims/448107/

Aji, M. P., Riadi, I., & Lutfhi, A. (2017, October 15). The Digital Forensic Analysis of Snapchat Application Using XML Records. *Journal of Theoretical and Applied Information Technology, 95*(19). Retrieved from http://www.jatit.org/volumes/Vol95No19/7Vol95No19.pdf

Alarms.org. (n.d.). *Burglary statistics: The hard numbers of home invasion.* Retrieved from www.alarms.org: https://www.alarms.org/burglary-statistics/

Betts, A. (2018, March 23). *Password vs. PIN vs. Fingerprint: The Best Way to Lock Your Android Phone.* Retrieved from www.makeuseof.com: https://www.makeuseof.com/tag/lock-methods-android-phone/

Bisson, D. (2015, March 23). *5 Social Engineering Attacks to Watch Out For.* Retrieved from www.tripwire.com: https://www.tripwire.com/state-of-security/security-awareness/5-social-engineering-attacks-to-watch-out-for/

Bonneau, J., Bursztein, E., Caron, I., Jackson, R., & Williamson, M. (2015). Secrets, Lies, and Account Recovery: Lessons from the Use of Personal Knowledge Questions at Google. *WWW'15 - Proceedings of the 22nd international conference on World Wide Web, ACM (2015.* International World Wide Web Conference Committee. doi:http://dx.doi.org/10.1145/2736277.2741691

Boodaei, M. (2011, January 4). *Mobile Users 3 Times More Vulnerable to Phishing Attacks.* Retrieved from securityintelligence.com: https://securityintelligence.com/mobile-users-3-times-more-vulnerable-to-phishing-attacks/

Brewster, T. (2019, January 14). *Feds Can't Force You To Unlock Your iPhone With Finger Or Face, Judge Rules.* Retrieved from www.forbes.com:

https://www.forbes.com/sites/thomasbrewster/2019/01/14/feds-cant-force-you-to-unlock-your-iphone-with-finger-or-face-judge-rules/#3d41c22f42b7

Brown, S. L. (2017, November 13). *iPad generation's fingers not ready to write, teachers say.* Retrieved from www.abc.net.au: https://www.abc.net.au/news/2017-11-14/ipad-generations-fingers-not-ready-to-write/9143880

Brumley, D. (2019, January 29). *Mayhem, the Machine That Finds Software Vulnerabilities, Then Patches Them.* Retrieved from spectrum.ieee.org: https://spectrum.ieee.org/computing/software/mayhem-the-machine-that-finds-software-vulnerabilities-then-patches-them?utm_source=techalert&utm_campaign=techalert-02-07-19&utm_medium=email

Bursztein, E. (2015, May 21). *New Research: Some Tough Questions for 'Security Questions'* . Retrieved from security.googleblog.com: https://security.googleblog.com/2015/05/new-research-some-tough-questions-for.html

Cabrero, A. (2019, March 28). *'Virtual kidnapping' scam spreading across the country.* Retrieved from www.ksl.com: https://www.ksl.com/article/46519815/virtual-kidnapping-scam-spreading-across-the-country

Calyptix. (2018, April 13). *Top Causes of Data Breaches by Industry 2018: Verizon DBIR.* Retrieved from www.calyptix.com: https://www.calyptix.com/top-threats/top-causes-of-data-breaches-by-industry-2018-verizon-dbir/

Carleton University. (2016, May 2). *10 Tips to Stay Safe on Social Media.* Retrieved from https://carleton.ca/its/2016/social-media-safety/

Cass, S. (2019, March 6). *Ransomware Is So 2017: Modern Cybercriminals Are All About Cryptojacking.* Retrieved from spectrum.ieee.org: https://spectrum.ieee.org/tech-talk/telecom/security/ransomware-is-so-2017-modern-cybercriminals-are-all-about-cryptojacking

Cervantes, E. (2015, August 22). *Lock patterns are more predictable than we thought.* Retrieved from www.androidauthority.com:

https://www.androidauthority.com/lock-pattern-predictable-636267/

Chokey, A. (2019, February 10). *Miramar men among 3 accused in $80,000 'grandparent scam'.* Retrieved from www.sun-sentinel.com: https://www.sun-sentinel.com/news/crime/fl-ne-grandpa-scam-arrests-20190210-story.html

Collins, J. (2018, March 1). *Online security: The password-recovery questions you should be answering.* Retrieved from www.journalofaccountancy.com: https://www.journalofaccountancy.com/issues/2018/mar/password-recovery-questions.html

Collins, J. (2019, January 15). *What Are Cookies on a Computer?* Retrieved from www.lifewire.com: https://www.lifewire.com/web-browser-cookies-3483129

Coughlan, S. (2018, October 30). *Surgery students 'losing dexterity to stitch patients'.* Retrieved from www.bbc.com: https://www.bbc.com/news/education-46019429

Crane, J. (2019). *Wi-Fi Security Types.* Retrieved from support.metageek.com: https://support.metageek.com/hc/en-us/articles/200971094-Wi-Fi-Security-Types

Dayaratna, A. (2018, October). *IDC's Worldwide Developer Census, 2018: Part-Time Developers Lead the Expansion of the Global Developer Population.* Retrieved from www.idc.com: https://www.idc.com/research/viewtoc.jsp?containerId=US44363318

DeMille, D. (2019, January 31). *Will Your House Be Broken Into This Year?* Retrieved from www.asecurelife.com: https://www.asecurelife.com/burglary-statistics/

DHS. (n.d.). *Software Assurance.* Department of Homeland Security, DHS Cyber Security. Retrieved from www.us-cert.gov: https://www.us-cert.gov/sites/default/files/publications/infosheet_SoftwareAssurance.pdf

Eldridge, A. (n.d.). *What Comes After Terabyte?* Retrieved from www.britannica.com: https://www.britannica.com/story/what-comes-after-terabyte

Epstein, M. (2019, February 6). *Make Sure Your Passwords Stay Up to Date With This Google Chrome Extension.* Retrieved from lifehacker.com: https://lifehacker.com/make-sure-your-passwords-stay-up-to-date-with-this-goog-1832359833

Erickson, A. (n.d.). *Hide Your Keys In These Spots & You'll Get Robbed.* Retrieved from www.familyhandyman.com: https://www.familyhandyman.com/smart-homeowner/hide-your-keys-in-these-spots-youll-get-robbed/

Eyewitness Surveillance. (2017, MArch 30). *Where Americans Don't Lock Their Doors.* Retrieved from http://www.eyewitnesssurveillance.com: http://www.eyewitnesssurveillance.com/americans-dont-lock-doors-survey/

FCC. (2018, November 5). *CHAIRMAN PAI CALLS ON INDUSTRY TO ADOPT ANTI-SPOOFING PROTOCOLS TO HELP CONSUMERS COMBAT SCAM ROBOCALLS.* Retrieved from docs.fcc.gov: https://docs.fcc.gov/public/attachments/DOC-354933A1.pdf

FCC. (2019, March 4). *Caller ID Spoofing.* Retrieved from www.fcc.gov: https://www.fcc.gov/consumers/guides/spoofing-and-caller-id

FCC. (n.d.). *Combating Spoofed Robocalls with Caller ID Authentication.* Retrieved from www.fcc.gov: https://www.fcc.gov/call-authentication

Fellows, R. (2008, August). *Full, incremental or differential: How to choose the correct backup type.* Retrieved from searchdatabackup.techtarget.com: https://searchdatabackup.techtarget.com/feature/Full-incremental-or-differential-How-to-choose-the-correct-backup-type

Fletcher, E. (2018, December 3). *New twist to grandparent scam: mail cash.* Retrieved from www.ftc.gov: https://www.ftc.gov/news-events/blogs/data-spotlight/2018/12/new-twist-grandparent-scam-mail-cash

Fortney, L. (2019, February 10). *Bitcoin Mining, Explained.* Retrieved from www.investopedia.com: https://www.investopedia.com/terms/b/bitcoin-mining.asp

Fractional CISO. (2019, February 6). *Correct Horse Battery Staple Review – Password Advice.* Retrieved from fractionalciso.com: https://fractionalciso.com/correct-horse-battery-staple-review/

Frankenfield, J. (2019, February 12). *Cryptocurrency* . Retrieved from www.investopedia.com: https://www.investopedia.com/terms/c/cryptocurrency.asp

Gerhardt, N. (n.d.). *35 Things You're Doing That Make Your House a Target for Burglars.* Retrieved from www.rd.com: https://www.rd.com/home/improvement/house-a-target-for-burglars/

Giusti, A. C. (2018, March 27). *Chip-and-skin: Payments' Matrix moment.* Retrieved from www.paymentssource.com: https://www.paymentssource.com/news/chip-and-skin-implantable-rfid-gives-payments-its-matrix-moment

Goodin, D. (2015, august 20). *New data uncovers the surprising predictability of Android lock patterns.* Retrieved from arstechnica.com: https://arstechnica.com/information-technology/2015/08/new-data-uncovers-the-surprising-predictability-of-android-lock-patterns/

Graham, J. (2017, August 9). *You will get chipped — eventually.* Retrieved from www.usatoday.com: https://www.usatoday.com/story/tech/2017/08/09/you-get-chipped-eventually/547336001/

Grassi, P. A., Fenton, J. L., Newton, E. M., Perlner, R. A., Regenscheid, A. R., Burr, W. E., . . . Theofanos, M. F. (2017, June). *Digital Identity Guidelines.* National Institute of Standards and Technology, Gaithersburg, MD. doi:doi.org/10.6028/NIST.SP.800-63b

Hampson, M. (2019, February 8). *LipPass Authenticates Users Based On the Way They Move Their Mouths.* Retrieved from spectrum.ieee.org: https://spectrum.ieee.org/tech-talk/consumer-electronics/gadgets/this-new-approach-for-user-identification-allows-phones-to-read-your-lips

Happ, C., Melzer, A., & Steffgen, G. (2016, August). Trick with treat – Reciprocity increases the willingness to communicate personal data. *Computers in Human Behavior, Volume 61*, pp. 372-377. doi:10.1016/j.chb.2016.03.026

Herrick, K. (2017, June 20). *Best Shredders: Top Five Picks for Maximum Security.* Retrieved from www.asecurelife.com: https://www.asecurelife.com/best-shredders/

Hill, A. (2018, February 25). *Children struggle to hold pencils due to too much tech, doctors say.* Retrieved from www.theguardian.com: https://www.theguardian.com/society/2018/feb/25/children-struggle-to-hold-pencils-due-to-too-much-tech-doctors-say

Holpuch, A. (2013, May 9). *Deleted Snapchat photos recovered 'within days' by forensics company.* Retrieved from www.theguardian.com: https://www.theguardian.com/technology/2013/may/09/snapchat-photos-not-deleted

IBM Security. (2019). *X-Force Threat Intelligence Index 2019.* Armonk, NY: IBM Corporation. Retrieved March 13, 2019, from https://www.ibm.com/downloads/cas/ZGB3ERYD

Johansen, A. G. (n.d.). *7 Steps to Take Right After a Data Breach.* Retrieved from www.lifelock.com: https://www.lifelock.com/learn-data-breaches-steps-to-take-right-after-a-data-breach.html

La Rosa, L. (2018, October 2). *Recent string of celebrity home burglaries linked to social media posts: Police.* Retrieved from abcnews.go.com: https://abcnews.go.com/Entertainment/recent-string-celebrity-home-burglaries-linked-social-media/story?id=58230153

Leyden, J. (2003, April 18). *Office workers give away passwords for a cheap pen.* Retrieved from www.theregister.co.uk: https://www.theregister.co.uk/2003/04/18/office_workers_give_away_passwords/

Lord, N. (2019, January 3). *Data Breach Experts Share The Most Important Next Step You Should Take After A Data Breach in 2019 & Beyond.* Retrieved from digitalguardian.com: https://digitalguardian.com/blog/data-breach-experts-share-most-important-next-step-you-should-take-after-data-breach-2014-2015

Lord, N. (2019, January 14). *Social Engineering Attacks: Common Techniques & How to Prevent an Attack.* Retrieved from digitalguardian.com: https://digitalguardian.com/blog/social-engineering-attacks-common-techniques-how-prevent-attack

McAfee. (2018, September). *McAfee Labs Threat Report: September 2018.* Retrieved from www.mcafee.com: https://www.mcafee.com/enterprise/en-us/assets/reports/rp-quarterly-threats-sep-2018.pdf

McMillan, R. (2017, August 7). *The Man Who Wrote Those Password Rules Has a New Tip: N3v$r M1^d!* Retrieved from www.wsj.com: https://www.wsj.com/articles/the-man-who-wrote-those-password-rules-has-a-new-tip-n3v-r-m1-d-1502124118

Middlebrook, H. (2016, October 21). *New screen time rules for kids, by doctors.* Retrieved from edition.cnn.com: https://edition.cnn.com/2016/10/21/health/screen-time-media-rules-children-aap/index.html

Monnappa, K. A. (2018). *Learning Malware Analysis.* Birmingham, UK: Packt Publishing.

Morgan, S. (2016, December 19). *World will need to secure 111 billion lines of new software code in 2017.* Retrieved from www.csoonline.com: https://www.csoonline.com/article/3151003/application-development/world-will-need-to-secure-111-billion-lines-of-new-software-code-in-2017.html

Morris, H. (2018, August 30). *Why social media posts could invalidate your home insurance.* Retrieved from /www.telegraph.co.uk: https://www.telegraph.co.uk/travel/advice/social-media-post-invalidate-insurance-burglary/

Mort, M., & Foss, J. (2016, April 12). *One New Zero-Day Discovered on Average Every Week in 2015, Twice the Rate of a Year Ago as Advanced Attackers Exploit, Stockpile and Resell High-Value Vulnerabilities.* Retrieved from investor.symantec.com: https://investor.symantec.com/About/Investors/press-releases/press-release-details/2016/One-New-Zero-Day-Discovered-on-Average-Every-Week-in-2015-Twice-the-Rate-of-a-Year-Ago-as-Advanced-Attackers-Exploit-Stockpile-and-Resell-High-Value-Vulnerabilities/de

National Crime Prevention Council. (n.d.). *Social Networking Safety.* Retrieved from http://archive.ncpc.org: http://archive.ncpc.org/topics/internet-safety/social-networking-safety.html

National Cybersecurity and Communications Integration Center. (2015, July 5). *Security Tip (ST06-003) Staying Safe on Social Networking Sites.* Retrieved from www.us-cert.gov: https://www.us-cert.gov/ncas/tips/ST06-003

NBC. (2016, August 22). *Some Burglars Using Social Media to Find Targets, I-Team Survey Shows.* Retrieved from www.nbcnewyork.com: https://www.nbcnewyork.com/news/local/Investigations-I-Team-Social-Media-Use-Survey-New-York-New-Jersey-390938211.html

Nikolov, G. (2018, June 26). *Why is Mobile Security Important?* Retrieved from vedc.org: https://vedc.org/blog/why-is-mobile-security-important

Norman, J. (n.d.). *Not Getting Gigabit Speeds?* Retrieved from sewelldirect.com: https://sewelldirect.com/learning-center/gigabit-speeds

Padia, R. (2015, May 26). *Google analyzes answers to common security questions.* Retrieved from androidcommunity.com: https://androidcommunity.com/google-analyzes-answers-to-common-security-questions-20150526/

Palmer, D. (2018, May 30). *What is malware? Everything you need to know about viruses, trojans and malicious software.* Retrieved from www.zdnet.com: https://www.zdnet.com/article/what-is-malware-everything-you-need-to-know-about-viruses-trojans-and-malicious-software/

Pettit, H., & Pinkstone, J. (2018, May 14). *Would you have a microchip implanted under your SKIN? 3,000 Swedes with electronic tags embedded into their hands risk their personal data being 'used against them'.* Retrieved from www.dailymail.co.uk: https://www.dailymail.co.uk/sciencetech/article-5726197/Would-microchip-SKIN-3-000-Swedes-electronic-tag-embedded-hands.html

Phillips, G. (2018, March 22). *10 Basic Encryption Terms Everyone Should Know and Understand.* Retrieved from www.makeuseof.com: https://www.makeuseof.com/tag/samsung-galaxy-s10-overview/

Phillips, G. (2019, January 16). *WEP vs. WPA vs. WPA2 vs. WPA3: Wi-Fi Security Types Explained* . Retrieved from www.makeuseof.com: https://www.makeuseof.com/tag/wep-wpa-wpa2-wpa3-explained/

Ponemon Institute. (2018, February). *2018 Study on Global Megatrends in Cybersecurity.* Retrieved from www.raytheon.com: https://www.raytheon.com/sites/default/files/2018-02/2018_Global_Cyber_Megatrends.pdf

Raphael, J. (2019, FEb 21). *7 mobile security threats you should take seriously in 2019.* Retrieved from www.csoonline.com: https://www.csoonline.com/article/3241727/7-mobile-security-threats-you-should-take-seriously-in-2019.html

Reavy, P. (2019, April 1). *Uncovering secret that led to son's suicide.* Retrieved from www.deseretnews.com: https://www.deseretnews.com/article/900063495/uncovering-secret-that-led-to-sons-suicide-utah-family-shares-story-sextortion.html

Reed, L. (2016, January 15). *Digital distraction in class is on the rise, study says.* Retrieved from phys.org: https://phys.org/news/2016-01-digital-distraction-class.html

Roberson, L. (2013, May 16). *Study Provides Insights on Habits and Motivations of Burglars.* Retrieved from news.uncc.edu: https://news.uncc.edu/news-events/news-releases/study-provides-insights-habits-and-motivations-burglars

Rogers, C. (2019, January 17). *Here's what screen time is doing to our brains.* Retrieved from www.ksl.com: https://www.ksl.com/article/46470624/heres-what-screen-time-is-doing-to-our-brains

Rosenbaum, C. (2018, October 4). *Celebrities Keep Getting Burglarized Because They Can't Help Themselves On Social Media.* Retrieved from www.buzzfeednews.com: https://www.buzzfeednews.com/article/claudiarosenbaum/celebrities-burglarized-social-media

Rouse, M. (2018, May). *Social engineering.* Retrieved from searchsecurity.techtarget.com: https://searchsecurity.techtarget.com/definition/social-engineering

Royal College of Paediatricss and Child Health. (2019, January 4). *Build screen time around family activities, not the other way round, parents told.* Retrieved from www.rcpch.ac.uk: https://www.rcpch.ac.uk/news-events/news/build-screen-time-around-family-activities-not-other-way-round-parents-told

Savoie, M. (2012). *Building Successful Information Systems: Five Best Practices to Ensure Organizational Effectiveness and Profitability.* New York, NY: Business Expert Press.

Seals, T. (2017, December 14). *360K New Malware Samples Hit the Scene Every Day.* Retrieved from www.infosecurity-magazine.com: https://www.infosecurity-magazine.com/news/360k-new-malware-samples-every-day/

Segarra, L. M. (2018, September 8). *Mac App Store Still Seems to Have Malicious Apps.* Retrieved from www.fortune.com: http://fortune.com/2018/09/08/mac-app-store-malware/

Shankland, S. (2018, October 3). *Here come Wi-Fi 4, 5 and 6 in plan to simplify 802.11 networking names.* Retrieved from www.cnet.com: https://www.cnet.com/news/wi-fi-alliance-simplifying-802-11-wireless-network-tech-names/

Silver, E. (2018, September 28). *Wireless Networking and Security Standards.* Retrieved from it.ucsf.edu: https://it.ucsf.edu/policies/wireless-networking-and-security-standards

Smith, A. (2018, September 21). *Free credit freezes are here.* Retrieved from www.consumer.ftc.gov: https://www.consumer.ftc.gov/blog/2018/09/free-credit-freezes-are-here

Sobers, R. (2019, January 7). *60 Must-Know Cybersecurity Statistics for 2019.* Retrieved from www.varonis.com: https://www.varonis.com/blog/cybersecurity-statistics/

Statista. (2019). *Number of mobile phone users worldwide from 2015 to 2020 (in billions).* Retrieved March 9, 2019, from www.statista.com: https://www.statista.com/statistics/274774/forecast-of-mobile-phone-users-worldwide/

Thomas, N. (2018, October 10). *Limiting children's screen time linked to better cognition, study says.* Retrieved from edition.cnn.com: https://edition.cnn.com/2018/09/26/health/screen-time-cognition-study/index.html

Trend Micro. (2017, October 10). *Best Practices: Securing Your Mobile Device.* Retrieved from www.trendmicro.com: https://www.trendmicro.com/vinfo/us/security/news/mobile-safety/best-practices-securing-your-mobile-device

U.S. Department of Education. (2005, February 17). *Protection of Pupil Rights Amendment (PPRA).* Retrieved from www2.ed.gov: https://www2.ed.gov/policy//gen/guid/fpco/ppra/index.html

U.S. General Services Administration. (2014, October 29). *GSA Rules of Behavior for Handling Personally Identifiable Information(PII).* Retrieved from www.gsa.gov: https://www.gsa.gov/cdnstatic/CIO_P2180.1_GSA_Rules_of_Behavior_for_Handling_Personally_Identifiable_Information_%28PII%29_%28Signed_on_October_29__2014%29.pdf

Université du Luxembourg. (2016, May 12). *Social engineering: Password in exchange for chocolate.* Retrieved from www.sciencedaily.com: https://www.sciencedaily.com/releases/2016/05/160512085123.htm

USA.gov. (2019, February 14). *Identity Theft.* Retrieved from www.usa.gov: https://www.usa.gov/identity-theft

Verger, R. (2017, June 1). *Intel's new chip puts a teraflop in your desktop. Here's what that means.* Retrieved from www.popsci.com: https://www.popsci.com/intel-teraflop-chip#page-2

Verizon. (2018, April). *2018 Data Breach Investigations Report, 11th edutuib.* Retrieved from enterprise.verizon.com: https://enterprise.verizon.com/resources/reports/DBIR_2018_Report.pdf

Warren, T. (2017, April 4). *Apple reveals Windows 10 is four times more popular than the Mac.* Retrieved from www.theverge.com: https://www.theverge.com/2017/4/4/15176766/apple-microsoft-windows-10-vs-mac-users-figures-stats

About the Author

Chris's first experience with computers was in the early 1980s with a friend's Commodore PET computer. They'd load a data cassette, wait while the program loaded into memory, and then play Space Invaders on the small green screen. Several years later, Chris's family purchased an Apple IIe computer, and he became the go-to person in the family for computer issues.

Chris enjoys the outdoors, particularly the mountains, and his first bachelor's degree was in recreation management and youth leadership. While single, he pursued various interests including becoming certified as a private helicopter pilot. He was also certified as an advanced ground school instructor and earned additional flight certifications while he taught ground school classes. When the helicopter company became a victim of the Great Recession, Chris enrolled in a multimedia design and development course.

His knack with computers and other tech quickly changed his part-time job functions from administrative assistant to tech, and it later became a full-time position. Chris enrolled in some IT classes, and he passed the CompTIA A+ and Security+ and Apple Certified Support Professional certifications.

During the next several years, Chris earned a network administration certificate, an associate of applied science in information systems and technology, an associate of applied science in business management, and a bachelor of science in information systems, with an emphasis in business intelligence.

Chris then completed a graduate certificate in cybersecurity and pursued a master's degree in cybersecurity.

While Chris enjoys learning, he prefers to spend time with his wife and four children whenever possible.

Thank you!

Once again, thank you for reading my book!

Your feedback is very much appreciated. I'm sure I've missed something or should've gone into more detail in some place and less detail in another. Other comments and suggestions are helpful as well. Your input is needed to make any future editions better. You can reach out through a review on Amazon, or on my website.

I'd also appreciate you taking a few moments to leave a helpful review on Amazon to let others know how you liked the book.

Thanks so much!

—Christopher Cox

www.ckcox.com

Printed in Great Britain
by Amazon

36713885R10149